A READER OF EARLY LIBERAL JUDAISM

D1460433

For my father

A Reader of Early Liberal Judaism

The Writings of Israel Abrahams, Claude Montefiore, Lily Montagu and Israel Mattuck

Selected, edited and introduced by
EDWARD KESSLER

VALLENTINE MITCHELL
LONDON • PORTLAND, OR

First published in 2004 in Great Britain by
VALLENTINE MITCHELL
Suite 314, Premier House, 112–114 Station Road
Edgware, Middlesex HA8 7BJ

and in the United States of America by
VALLENTINE MITCHELL
c/o ISBS, 920 NE 58th Avenue, Suite 300
Portland, Oregon 97213-3786

Website hhttp://www.vmbooks.com

British Library Cataloguing in Publication Data

A catalogue record for this book is available
from the British Library

ISBN 0-85303-592-X (cloth)
ISBN 0-85303-600-4 (paper)

Library of Congress Cataloging-in-Publication Data

A catalog record for this book is available
from the Library of Congress

Typeset in 11/13pt Palatino by Vitaset, Paddock Wood, Kent
Printed in Great Britain by
MPG Books Ltd, Bodmin, Cornwall

Contents

Preface

This book would not have been completed without the encouragement of a number of my friends, colleagues and family.

I would like to thank Rabbi John Rayner for his guidance and encouragement. Rabbi David Goldberg has also been a great support and suggested the book in the first place. Both are Emeritus Rabbis at the Liberal Jewish Synagogue in St John's Wood, the spiritual home of each of the four founders of Liberal Judaism.

I am grateful to Tunde Formadi for her typing and scanning skills as well as to my other colleagues at the Centre for the Study of Jewish–Christian Relations in Cambridge (CJCR), Debbie Patterson-Jones, Melanie Wright, Lucia Faltin and Maty Matyszak. Together we have created a marvellous forum for study and dialogue. CJCR is a young and dynamic institute, which has provided the ideal environment in which to compose this book.

Finally, I wish to thank my beloved wife Trish and our children, Shoshana, Asher and Eliana, who regularly remind me about the priorities in my life but also have the patience to give me the necessary time and space in which to write.

This book is dedicated to my father, William Kessler, currently President of the Liberal Jewish Synagogue, who has devoted much of his life to supporting and sustaining Liberal Judaism. He walks in the footsteps of Israel Abrahams, Claude Montefiore, Lily Montagu and Israel Mattuck and is a model to all fathers.

1

Introduction

Surprisingly little has been written about the origins of Liberal Judaism in England and there is no single work that examines why the movement was founded or how it developed. Even the contributions of the four founders of Liberal Judaism are rarely considered. It is true that both Claude Montefiore and Lily Montagu have been the subject of individual studies,[1] but neither Israel Abrahams nor Israel Mattuck has received serious attention.

It is my hope that this introduction to their life and writings will go some way to filling the gap and also to stimulating more detailed studies. In this work I have selected the key writings of the four founders to illustrate their thought as well as their contribution to Liberal Judaism in the UK. Because their writings are relatively unknown, some people might assume that their contributions were limited. Such an assumption would be erroneous. On the contrary, without the scholarly contributions of Abrahams, the astute leadership of Montefiore, the organisational abilities of Montagu and the pastoral dynamism of Mattuck, the Liberal Jewish movement would not exist today. Each made a contribution and each, to borrow a rabbinic term, was an *ish ma'aseh*, a person of action. The four founders of Liberal Judaism made an essential contribution without which the movement would have floundered.

Although their lives did not exactly correlate, their writings provide evidence of an ongoing mutual influence. For example, Israel Abrahams was the foremost scholar of his time and was greatly admired by Claude Montefiore. Together they edited a number of sermons and established the *Jewish Quarterly Review*, whose significance is underlined by the fact that it was the first English-speaking academic Jewish journal. Such was Abrahams' influence that Montefiore repeated many of his arguments and referred to him as a student would to a teacher.

Montefiore's influence on Montagu was similarly profound and long-lasting. Although Montefiore died in 1938, Lily Montagu often referred to him as her teacher and guide. Montefiore's influence on Montagu can be seen in her writings, which often repeat Montefiore almost word for word. Montefiore's influence is also illustrated by Montagu's contribution to the establishment of Liberal Judaism. Montagu was prompted by Montefiore to write in 1899 an article that called for an association of Jews. This provided the catalyst for creation of Liberal Judaism in the UK. Yet the association for which Montagu appealed was only formed three years later. Why the delay? Because Montagu spent those three years cajoling Montefiore to take on the leadership of the nascent Liberal Jewish community, called the Jewish Religious Union (JRU). In other words, she delayed the creation of the JRU until he agreed to her request in 1902.

Montefiore was also a significant influence upon Israel Mattuck, since he persuaded Mattuck to leave a comfortable pulpit in New York State and take the reins at the first Liberal synagogue in England. Although Mattuck came to know Montefiore only during the latter stages of his life, he often acknowledged Montefiore's influence and dedicated one of his books to him. Mattuck is probably the least well known of the four founders, and a detailed study of his life and thought is sorely needed. It was Mattuck who galvanised the small Liberal Jewish community, based around one synagogue, and transformed it into a community of synagogues. As will be evident from the selection of writings, it was Mattuck who implemented a number of changes almost as soon as he arrived. His oft-commented-upon energy, as well as his ability to motivate leaders such as Lily Montagu, ensured that he attained a place alongside the other founders of Liberal Judaism.

HISTORICAL CONTEXT

The writings of the four need to be read in the context of nineteenth-century Victorian life. During that time the essential institutions of the Anglo-Jewish community were being established. For example, the *Jewish Chronicle* was launched in 1841, Jews' College was founded in 1855 and a few years later the United Synagogue came into existence as an amalgam of

Orthodox synagogues in central London. In 1871 the Anglo-Jewish Association was founded for the protection of Jews in poor and backward countries, and in 1888 the *Jewish Quarterly Review* started publication.

In the nineteenth and early twentieth centuries Anglo-Jewry was a compact and well-organised community. Its lay leaders, consisting primarily of members of the Montefiore, Goldsmid, Rothschild, Cohen, Montagu families (appropriately identified by Chaim Bermant as The Cousinhood[2]), were supported by a remarkable group of public servants such as Asher Asher at the United Synagogue, Abraham Benisch of the *Jewish Chronicle*, Solomon Almosnino at Bevis Marks and Albert Lowy at the Anglo-Jewish Association. During this time some Jews had also attained prominence in the social life of the country, and the participation of the brothers Sassoon and Rothschild in the 'Marlborough House Set' demonstrated the easy mix of Jews in almost every level of society.

The two most well-known figures in English society were Benjamin Disraeli and Moses Montefiore. Disraeli (1804–81), Prime Minister of Britain, was born a Jew but baptised when he was 12 years old. His affection for Jews and Judaism was known and accepted by the general public. Montefiore (1784–1885) also enjoyed widespread support. In particular, he was acclaimed for his action in response to the 1840 Damascus Affair, when Jews of the city were forced to face the medieval charge of ritual murder. Montefiore went to Damascus and procured the release and unconditional acquittal of the prisoners. On his return he was proclaimed a national hero and was granted an audience with Queen Victoria.

Towards the end of the century there occurred the first major wave of Jewish immigration, notably from Russia, the result of the pogroms that rocked the Jewish communities in Eastern Europe. From a population of 65,000 in 1880, the number of Jews increased to 300,000 in 1914. The communal leadership sought to 'anglicise' the immigrants, who had quickly established a network of institutions such as Yiddish newspapers, fraternity societies and trade unions. The United Synagogue was concerned with the preservation of Judaism in an English milieu, through a framework of a large modern English organisation and by synagogues of the Western model. The Anglo-Jewish model did not appeal to many of the Jewish immigrants who felt that the traditional Orthodox life of Eastern Europe would be best preserved by reflecting the atmosphere of the Eastern European communities (*kehillot*). In 1887 Samuel Montagu (Lord Swaythling) helped form the Federation of Synagogues, which was slightly more traditional than the United Synagogue and based upon the small synagogue.

The influx of such vast numbers perhaps not surprisingly resulted in an adverse reaction on the part of the local population. From 1905 immigration was restricted by various acts of parliament, and the outbreak of the First World War completely ended the great immigration.

In 1917, with the advent of the Balfour Declaration, Anglo-Jewry was promoted to a new and more important role in world Jewry as Great Britain became the administrative power for a Jewish national home. The community was completely divided about the benefits to Judaism of political Zionism. Some of the community were in favour of the Zionist aspirations but there other some influential leaders, such as Claude Montefiore and Lord Swaything (Lily Montagu's father), who did all that was in their power to prevent the realisation of a Jewish state.

The 1920s were a relatively quiet period marked mainly by the geographical shift of the population, while the 1930s were overshadowed by the rise of fascism in Europe. This produced the second major wave of immigration. Once again the Jewish population increased and by 1950 it was estimated to be in the region of 450,000 people. Although the increase was not as great as that at the turn of the century the effects were as dramatic: these new immigrants were mainly middle-class Jews, unlike their proletarian brothers and sisters of the first wave. They contributed to a resurgence of Jewish religious and social life. For example, ministers and scholars trained in European Reform movements revitalised Progressive Judaism; the Frankfurt-inspired Orthodox expanded the Orthodox movement and produced a shift to the right in the United Synagogue.

Continental racism also crossed the Channel and under the English fascist leader, Oswald Mosley, provocative marches were led through predominantly Jewish areas. These marches did, however, have one major positive benefit: the need for self-defence produced a strong feeling of solidarity within the Jewish community.

LIBERAL JUDAISM IN ENGLAND

The movement to reform Judaism started in Germany in the early nineteenth century with leaders such as Israel Jacobson. Most commonly called Reform Judaism, the movement was also known as Liberal and Progressive Judaism. Its dynamism varied from place to place, undergoing constant change in the course of time. Conservative and radical positions co-existed and all groups shared the assertion of the legitimacy of change in Judaism and the denial of eternal validity of any given formulation of Jewish belief or codification of Jewish law. Apart from that, it must be said, there was (and still is) little agreement.

At the beginning the most noticeable demands of the reformers were associated with prayer and the synagogue. Various reforms were suggested, including:

- shortening the liturgy;
- reciting some of the prayers in the vernacular ;
- introducing choral singing with organ accompaniment; and
- delivering the sermon on Sabbaths.

The first major synagogue embodying these reforms was founded at Hamburg in 1818. Soon afterwards, some of the leading scholars and rabbis of the time, among them Abraham Geiger, came to the support of the movement and by the 1840s it had spread successfully to the shores of America.

In Britain, unlike Germany and the United States, the reform of Judaism was a plant of slow growth and when the subject of change was initially broached it met with bitter opposition. Thus the Spanish and Portuguese congregation of London did everything they could to prevent the organisation of a Reform synagogue. As soon as it was established in 1841, the West London Synagogue of British Jews was denounced as schismatic and a warning was issued against its endorsement to all the Jewish congregations in England. The chief rabbis of the two Orthodox wings promulgated an order against all members of the Reform Synagogue, and an excommunication (*herem*) was issued against them. Excommunicated they could not, for example, be buried in the cemetery of their parents but had to acquire one of their own. However, only a few years later, in 1849, the ban was lifted, signalling the community's acceptance of the reformers.

Although the Reform synagogue survived its condemnation it continued primarily as a congregation rather than a movement. Later a new congregation was formed in Manchester and another in Bradford; but no further ritual changes were introduced. The three synagogues all retained their conservative character and their reforms were not as radical as those in Germany (although they included an English sermon and an abridged Hebrew liturgy). This was probably because the West London Synagogue was founded for social reasons rather than theological – the Jews involved had moved from the East End of London, a poor immigrant area, to the more prosperous West End. They wanted to establish a branch synagogue that was geographically closer to them, rather than desiring a reform.

The lack of growth of English Reform was partly the result of the actions of Moses Montefiore, who was totally opposed to any reform and spent a great deal of his life preventing the movement from making an impact upon Anglo-Jewry. Towards the end of the century, however, sporadic attempts were made to provide supplementary religious services for the community, and this can be seen as a turning point for the Reform movement.

In 1890, at West Hampstead Town Hall, a Saturday afternoon service was started in order to attract those who found no spiritual satisfaction in the existing services. Morris Joseph, the religious leader, was accompanied by Claude Montefiore, who was one of a few laymen who delivered occasional sermons. The movement had to face the continued objection of the chief rabbi and the services, after making little headway, were abandoned three years later. Soon afterwards a new, more controversial group under the leadership of Oswald J. Simon sprang up. It was called 'The Sunday Movement' since it offered services on Sunday mornings as well as Sabbath services on Saturdays. Its intent was not only to gain religious interest among Jews but also to propagate Judaism actively among non-Jews. While 60 people showed up at the first service (most of them non-Jewish), there was once again insufficient support for the group to survive.

A few years later, in 1899, Liberal Judaism began to establish its roots in the country. Lily Montagu, on the suggestion of Claude Montefiore, wrote an article for the *Jewish Quarterly Review* entitled, 'The Spiritual Possibilities in Judaism today'.

This article began the process that eventually led to the formation of Liberal Judaism. It evoked a favourable response from several communal leaders, including Orthodox ministers, and encouraged Lily Montagu to believe that there was a significant number of Jews who shared liberal views. Montagu herself made it clear that she simply wanted to create an association of Reform and Orthodox Jews, which would contribute to the revival of Judaism. Its purpose, she explained in a letter outlining the reasons in favour of such a development, was to help Anglo-Jewry progress by revitalising the religious life of the community. An initial meeting took place in November 1901, when it was proposed that a new religious organisation should be founded under the name Jewish Religious Union (JRU), and the first official meeting took place in February of the next year.

The leadership committee consisted of ten members including three from the United Synagogue: Henrietta Franklin, A. A. Green, Albert Jessel, Morris Joseph, N. S. Joseph, Lily Montagu, Claude Montefiore, Oswald Simon, Simeon Singer and Isadore Spielman. The group agreed to institute special supplementary services to be held on Saturday afternoons 'conducted on lines specially adapted to the requirements of those to whom the present synagogue services ordinarily fail to appeal'.[3]

The first service took place on 1 October 1902. It was led by Simeon Singer (Israel Abraham's father-in-law) and Claude Montefiore gave the address. The *Jewish Chronicle*, which reported the service quoted him as follows:

> We believe that there are many Jews and Jewesses who seldom or never attend a place of worship ... now the causes are many and various ... but among them we believe one cause to be that many Jews and Jewesses do not like the kind of services which are open for them to attend.[4]

Between three and four hundred people attended, and services continued to attract large numbers. The Chief Rabbi and Orthodox leaders, including Lily Montagu's father, soon bitterly attacked the Union, accusing it of being a 'menace to Judaism' and schismatic in intent.

The JRU did not see itself as an attempt to establish a rival Jewish movement, competing with the Orthodox synagogues.

Learning perhaps from the experience of previous Reform attempts when synagogues were established, it did not intend to found a separate synagogue, and although many of the leading spirits of the movement were 'liberal' in their religious beliefs, this was not the case as regards the entire number of those who composed its governing body. It was, in its early days and years, a union of men and women who belonged to different platforms, but who all agreed that there was need for services that should in many respects differ from the services of the ordinary synagogues.

However, this utopian ideal of a broad movement consisting of different views could not endure. The Orthodox ministers were pressured into resigning and the Union, without having the base a synagogue might provide, began to lose the interest of the community. In 1909 it was argued that the establishment of a Liberal Jewish congregation (although forbidden by the original charter of the JRU) would be a suitable response to these problems. The majority of the members agreed that the establishment of a Liberal Jewish congregation was the only hope for the survival of a 'liberal' view of Judaism. The goal of revitalising Jewish religious life without becoming a separate Liberal Jewish organisation had, for all practical purposes, failed. This failure marked the end of the first stage in the creation of Liberal Judaism because it forced the leaders to reconsider their position and eventually to look overseas for guidance.

The second stage began in 1912 with the purchase of a site for a synagogue and the visit of Claude Montefiore to America with Charles Singer. Their goal was to find a rabbi who would lead the congregation and provide leadership to reformers throughout the country. They returned to London with Israel Mattuck, who agreed to lead the community at the Liberal Jewish Synagogue. From that point on, the JRU (later called the Jewish Religious Union for the Advancement of Liberal Judaism) started to develop and Liberal Judaism expanded to become a significant influence in Anglo-Jewish life.

During the next quarter-century, the growth of liberal Judaism in terms of the number of adherents and new synagogues was matched by the publication of a prolific number of books and articles, the majority of which were written by Israel Abrahams and Claude Montefiore. By the time of Montefiore's death in 1938, Liberal Judaism had established itself as a significant force in Anglo-Jewry. Mattuck and Montagu, whose contributions continued for some decades, were greatly influenced by the writings of Abrahams and Montefiore. Montagu, in particular, remained heavily in debt to Montefiore.

The four founders of Liberal Judaism had much in common. Their work and their lives were impelled by their faith in Judaism, in humanity and in their search for truth. They all passionately believed in Judaism and in the Jewish people. They wanted Jews to be Jewish in the religious sense and wanted Judaism to possess the depth and breadth of which they believed it was capable. They believed passionately in truth and in its ultimate triumph. They wanted Judaism to embody truth as much as possible, and employed human reason as a means of evaluation. They also passionately believed in the dignity of human beings and in the ability of mankind to attain redemption. They believed that they had to address themselves to all humanity and wanted Judaism to become a universal faith. For the four founders, all these reasons inevitably led to Liberal Judaism.

Israel Abrahams (1858–1925)

Abrahams, the earliest of the four, was recognized by Orthodox and Liberal Jew alike as the foremost Anglo-Jewish scholar of his day. The JRU pointed to its 'three Ms' – Montefiore, Montagu and Mattuck – yet all three were dependent upon the scholarship of Israel Abrahams.

Abrahams was born into a distinguished and scholarly family. His father, Barnett, was born in Warsaw, and was honorary *hacham* of London's Spanish and Portuguese congregation and headmaster of Jews' College School. His father-in-law, Simeon Singer, was editor of the Orthodox prayer book. Israel's grasp of Jewish learning was recognized at a young age, and he became the first graduate of Jews' College to receive an MA degree from the University of London. He was appointed senior tutor at Jews' College in 1881 and remained there until his move in 1902 to Cambridge, where he became Reader in Rabbinics.

During his time in Cambridge he influenced a generation of students, both Jews and Christians, especially those who had been brought up with a traditional Jewish education and who were uncomfortable in the face of the new teachings (such as biblical criticism) and suffered from crises of faith. One of his students, Herbert Loewe, who later also became Reader in Rabbinics at Cambridge, explained Abrahams' influence on Jewish students as follows:

> We consulted the recognised Jewish authorities but the answers we received in no wise [sic] solved our perplexities. Only Abrahams could understand, sympathize and help. By his teaching we learnt how to reconcile the old and the new. Through his help not merely our Judaism but our orthodoxy was strengthened. But for him several of us would have drifted far from our conservatism: through him we emerged from the conflict with firmer faith. Of all his pupils but one became a Liberal [... which] serves to prove the service Abrahams rendered to orthodoxy.[5]

One of Abrahams' great concerns was the futility of schism, and he complained that the tragedy of modern Judaism lay in its wasted effort – the desire for mutual understanding, he argued, had been powerfully and not infrequently voiced by different sides, but never simultaneously. He earnestly laboured for cooperation between different Jewish positions and was impatient with intolerant reform and bigoted orthodoxy alike. His message rings true today.

He called for Judaism to transcend narrow sectarian divides and also to be open to new and outside developments. He argued that Jewish tradition is a chain of many links, some of which are pure gold and others of inferior metals. Thus, he said, if 'we remove the latter [inferior metals], the chain will still hold, so long as we weld the remaining links honestly and add links of durable and genuine metal'.[6] Abrahams was primarily interested in the inner life of Jews and Judaism, believing that exposure to and interaction with outside cultures enhanced the inner vitality of Judaism. In addition to his numerous and significant publications, Abrahams was founder of the Jewish Historical Society of England, co-editor and co-founder of the *Jewish Quarterly Review*[7] with Claude Montefiore, and an early supporter of the Hebrew University in Jerusalem.

Although Abrahams was an eminent scholar who was respected by the academic fraternity, his name also became well known to the general public far away from the main academic centres of learning. For example, he contributed hundreds of articles to the *Jewish Chronicle*, a number of which are included in this book.

When the JRU was founded, Abrahams became a leading member of the governing body, causing him to resign his position at Jews' College. Montefiore and Abrahams were already close friends when Lily Montagu persuaded them both to support her initiative. Since he was such a respected scholar, his support for Liberal Judaism was of great importance in the early stages of the movement. No one could argue that Liberal Judaism simply represented a desire for convenience, for the reply was so obvious: what about Israel Abrahams?

Abrahams ensured that Liberal Jews understood that there were aspects to Orthodox Judaism that should be cherished. He made Liberal Jews perceive the similarities as well as the differences and realise in the differences legitimate developments, not haphazard changes. In sum, he remained a mediator between old and new, pointing out the errors of drawing a sharp line between biblical and rabbinic laws and objecting to the more extreme form of radical reform.

Like Montefiore, he made Rabbinic and Orthodox Judaism better understood by non-Jews. In Cambridge, his predecessor, Solomon Schechter, had understandably spent a great deal of his time on examining the Genizah collection, but when Abrahams took up his position in 1902 he succeeded in spreading knowledge of rabbinic Judaism within the University. In Professor Burkitt's famous seminar, which took place at the Faculty of Divinity, Abrahams ensured there was a desire to hear Jewish points of view; as a result he became an intermediary between Christian and Jewish learning as well as between Christian and Jewish scholars.

Claude Montefiore (1858–1938)

Claude Montefiore was born the year in which Lionel Roths-child became the first Jew to take his seat in the House of Commons. Montefiore's father was a nephew of Moses Montefiore and his mother a daughter of Isaac Goldsmid, one of the founders of the non-sectarian University College, London, and also of the West London Reform Synagogue.

Montefiore studied at Balliol College, Oxford, and came under the wing of Benjamin Jowett, who was to be a lasting influence upon him. Jowett encouraged Montefiore to devote himself to Judaism, and once wrote:

> I cannot advise you for or against the ministry, but I would certainly advise you to lead an ideal life, by which I mean a life not passed in the ordinary pleasures and pursuits of mankind; but in something higher, the study of your own people and their literature, and the means of elevating them. No life will make you as happy as that.[8]

Upon obtaining a first-class degree in 1889, he went to the Hochschule in Berlin with the intention of becoming a rabbi. There he was assigned to a young tutor by the name of Solomon Schechter, who was already an outstanding biblical and talmudic scholar. Schechter formed quite a contrast to his student – a native of Romania, from a family, who received a yeshiva education at a famous talmudic college at Lemberg (Lwow) in Galacia.

The two greatly respected each other's abilities. Schechter was amazed at the ease with which Montefiore grasped the meaning of difficult texts, and the student was so impressed with his tutor that he persuaded Schechter to return to England with him to continue his education. Just a few years later, in 1892, Schechter received the attention he deserved when he was appointed Reader in Rabbinics at Cambridge.

Montefiore started his first major scholarly exercise when he was invited to deliver the Hibbert Lectures in 1892: he was the first Jewish scholar to receive this honour. Schechter's influence upon Montefiore at this period is illustrated by his admission that 'to Schechter I owe more than I can adequately express. My whole conception of the Law and of its place in the Jewish religion and life is largely the fruit of his teaching and inspiration, while most of the rabbinical material on which that conception rests was put before my notice and explained to me by him.'[9]

The lectures were one of the first Jewish attempts to interpret the history of the Bible in accordance with the conclusions of 'Higher and Lower' criticism.[10] They attracted enormous attention because Montefiore:

1. accepted many of the results of modern scholarship;
2. paid tribute to the teachings of Jesus; and
3. vigorously defended Judaism from Christian criticism concerning the Torah.

In the Jewish community the benefit of Montefiore's response to Christian criticism outweighed any sense of alarm that his opposition to the Mosaic authorship of the Pentateuch and the value of the Synoptic Gospels might have aroused. Like Abrahams, Montefiore was concerned in his dealings with Christian scholars to respond to the negative portrayal of rabbinic Judaism. They were joined by Schechter, and the three argued against Christian polemic as illustrated by the influential writing of Emil Schürer, whose polemical description of 'life under the Law' in *History of the Jewish People in the Time of Jesus Christ* received justifiable notoriety. Montefiore made a significant contribution to the Christian reassessment of Jews and Judaism, and his criticism of prejudicial Christian scholarship received widespread support from scholars and leaders within both communities.

Throughout his life he attempted to build bridges and emphasise the positive value of the subject of study – rarely the negative. His biblical studies, for example, are based upon the view that the essence of the Bible is most truly shown at its best, and not at its worst; its true tendency and issue are displayed not in Esther, but in Jonah.

Following standard Victorian interpretation of scripture, Montefiore felt free to compare what he saw as more 'primitive' or 'lower' elements with 'higher' aspects. He concluded that the Bible contained the highest truth, but that it did not contain all truth. No book could be completely true in word and thought. The Bible was built up during several generations and different sections revealed different degrees of knowledge, faith and culture. This did not diminish the value of the Bible, but rather undermined the traditional Jewish understanding of it as perfect and divine. According to Montefiore, the Bible was divine because of its 'religious excellence' and because of its effects for 'righteousness and truth'. In other words, the Bible's value did not depend upon its divinity, but its divinity depended upon its value and excellence.

Montefiore was a man of independent means, for he had

inherited a large fortune from his father, brother (who died from rheumatic fever while travelling in America in 1879) and father-in-law. He was therefore able to devote himself to scholarship, but much of his time was spent on philanthropy. In particular he supported the Froebel Institute, the board of which he joined in 1882 as honorary secretary. Shortly afterwards he became its chairman. It was largely due to his help that the Froebel Institute was able to establish a permanent home at Grove House, Roehampton. He also was a benefactor of Hartley College, which later developed into the University of Southampton. He was president from 1913 to 1934 and made innumerable gifts to the college, such as an eleven-acre site that became the centre for its sporting activities. Most important of all for this study was Montefiore's leadership of and financial support for Liberal Judaism. His Liberal Jewish views formed the basis of all his writings, and Liberal Judaism was the main recipient of his practical encouragement and support.

Lily Montagu (1873–1963)

Lily Montagu was the sixth child of Samuel Montagu and Ellen Montagu (née Cohen). She was educated at a private school by tutors and raised in a traditional Orthodox home.

Throughout the second half of the nineteenth century the equality of women's education improved considerably, and by end of the century both Cambridge and Oxford permitted women to take their local examinations. While such openings benefited only a small percentage of women, upper-class girls such as Lily Montagu could take advantage of educational opportunities. Within Anglo-Jewry as a whole the emergence of the 'new woman' led to a re-evaluation of women's work and new opportunities. For instance, by the 1890s Jewish women were beginning to serve as members of a variety of communal organizations such as the Jewish Board of Guardians, and in 1902 a Conference of Jewish Women was held in London.

At the age of 17 Lily Montagu began pioneering work in the field of social services and with her sister Marian began to run evening classes for working girls and Sabbath services for children. She was 19 when she founded, with her cousin Beatrice, the West Central Club, an educational club for working girls. This was the first educational and social club formed for

Jewish girls of the working classes. The British club movement was in its infancy at that time, and the club leaders were amateurs trying to develop ways to respond to the needs of the working classes. The club developed into the West Central Jewish Day Settlement, with Lily remaining director into the 1960s.

Lily Montagu ensured that the West Central Club was based upon religious principles. Unlike Marian, Lily's concerns included the religious life and she sought to infuse the club with that spirit. While she was aware that the club members were, for the most part, religiously indifferent, she devoted much time to bringing to them an awareness of God.

During her life, Lily was a pioneer of the Youth Club Movement and founder of the National Organization of Girls' Clubs, and she was one of the first women in England to become a magistrate. She fought for decent conditions in sweat shops and helped open the way for the appointment of factory inspectors. During the Nazi period she helped refugees to escape Europe by securing entry permits.

The founding of the JRU in 1902 marked her formal entrance into the Anglo-Jewish community as a religious organizer, although as early as 1890 she had assumed a position of religious leadership and began to function as a lay preacher, holding services for children on Saturday mornings. This received the approval of Chief Rabbi Hermann Adler.

Interestingly, the opponents of the JRU acknowledged the right of women to participate in public religious life. Consequently, they aimed their attacks solely at the Union's theological foundations and not at the participation of women. As women began to play a more meaningful role with more visible functions within the Anglican Church so Jewish women began to achieve new religious roles as well. Since the Anglo-Jewish elite prided themselves on their Englishness they were receptive to new ideas about women's proper role within the Church and more broadly within Victorian religion.

Within the JRU Lily Montagu's chief contributions were organizational, but she sometimes did fulfil functions of religious leadership. For example, she assumed some of the roles in the JRU that she had already carried out at the Jewish Girls' Club – leading services, preaching sermons, teaching Bible classes and serving as an administrator. Anglo-Jewry's willingness to accord women greater communal responsibility facilitated her achievement of prominence within the public sphere of Jewish life.

Montagu acknowledged the writings and leadership of Claude Montefiore and the personal guidance of Israel Mattuck. She often referred to them as her teachers and inspiration, stating that she was implementing their ideas, not her own. It was Mattuck who convinced Lily Montagu that women were qualified to serve not only as religious organizers but also as religious leaders. At his insistence she preached her first sermon at the Liberal Jewish Synagogue (LJS) in 1915, and she was a regular preacher from then on. She also had her own congregation, the West Central Jewish Congregation, where she officiated every week and preached regularly.

Nevertheless, the greater influence was that of Montefiore, which began in her late teens and lasted throughout her life. Her view of Judaism as a personal religion based upon a relationship between the individual Jew and God was identified by Montefiore as Liberal Judaism. For his part, Montefiore greatly admired her ability to 'get things done' and she first came to his notice with the establishment of the West Central Club. His influence pervades her writings, which consist of articles, pamphlets and 14 books (most on religious subjects, but also three novels), and she may aptly be described as Montefiore's disciple.

Israel Mattuck (1883–1954)

Israel Mattuck was born to Lithuanian Orthodox Jews in 1883 who soon after his birth emigrated to the United States. He studied Semitics at Harvard University and came under influence of George Foot Moore, one of the greatest non-Jewish rabbinic scholars of his time. In 1905 he began his rabbinic studies at Cincinnati; he was ordained in 1910.

His first pulpit was in Rockaway, New York, and it was there that he met Claude Montefiore and Charles Singer. The leaders of the American Reform Movement had recommended Mattuck to Montefiore and Singer, who were sufficiently impressed to offer the young rabbi the pulpit of the Liberal Jewish Synagogue, which had just been established, and a position of leadership in the Liberal Jewish movement.

In January 1912 he was inducted into the LJS and made an immediate impression. Religion classes were organised and the first confirmation classes in Anglo-Jewish history were held for boys and girls aged 16. After the First World War, full equality was granted to women and, at his suggestion, Lily Montagu became the first woman to be invited to preach from the pulpit.

Soon after the liberal community grew beyond the means of Hill Street, Mattuck became involved in securing funds and a new site in St John's Wood. In 1925 the new synagogue was consecrated. In his consecration he explained the purpose, as he saw it, of Liberal Judaism, which was to 'show that Judaism is not an historic faith, but a living faith; that it can assimilate modern thought, and that it has a message for our times'.

Mattuck's views aroused much controversy in the Jewish community. For example, he described *kashrut* as an ancient Jewish prejudice, and enabled divorced Jewish women who had not received a *get* (legal bill of divorce) from their husbands to marry in the LJS. He was also vehemently opposed to Zionism, arguing that it was necessary to separate religion and nationality.

Mattuck, like Montefiore, became a spokesman of Judaism to the non-Jewish world. While Montefiore directed his energies towards tackling prejudice and ignorance in Christian scholarship, Mattuck was better known for his articles in the general press and his broadcasts. He engaged in dialogue with Christians and Christian clergy and was intimately involved in the establishment of the London Society of Jews and Christians, which paved the way for the creation of the Council of Christians and Jews in 1942.

Mattuck, unlike Montefiore and Abrahams, was not a prolific writer. He devoted his life to the development of Liberal Judaism and wrote only a few books and articles. Many of his writings and sermons remain unpublished. Nevertheless, what he wrote was significant and played an important role in the development of Liberal Judaism in England. He was also deeply involved in the publication of a new liberal prayer book and the development of a new liberal liturgy. One must also remember that of the four founders Mattuck was the most deeply involved in the running and organisation of synagogue life.

One of the most important themes of his writings concerns the mission of the Jewish people. In his view, Jews were a people of religion and by their continued existence as a dispersed yet distinct community they were able to demonstrate the power of religion to the world. They have a distinctive contribution to make to the religious life and thought of humanity. To fulfil their mission Jews must give to religion the supreme place in their earthly existence. In his view, Jews need to become more Jewish in order that humanity should become more religious.

NOTES

1. Edward Kessler, *An English Jew: The Life and Writings of Claude Montefiore*, London: Vallentine Mitchell (1988); E. Umansky, *Lily Montagu and the Advancement of Liberal Judaism*, New York: Edwin Mellen (1984).
2. Chaim Bermant, *The Cousinhood*, London: Eyre & Spottiswoode (1971).
3. Minutes of the JRU Committee 1902–1909 (meeting 16 February 1902), LJS Archives.
4. From Claude Montefiore's address at the first JRU service. *Jewish Chronicle*, 15 July 1938, p. 15.
5. Herbert Loewe, *Israel Abrahams*, Cambridge: Arthur Davis Memorial Trust (1944), p. 67.
6. Israel Abrahams (with Claude Montefiore), *Aspects of Judaism*, London: Macmillan.
7. In 1910 the work became too much for the editors and all rights were transferred to Dropsie College in Philadelphia, where it is still published today.
8. Lucy Cohen, *Some Recollections of Claude Montefiore*, London: Faber and Faber (1940), p. 47.
9. Claude Montefiore, *The Hibbert Lectures on the Origin and Growth of Religion as Illustrated by the Ancient Hebrews*, London: Williams and Norgate (1892).
10. Lower criticism examined the text, comparing it with and correcting it against the ancient manuscripts. Higher criticism inquired into the authorship and dates of different books and weighed their value as historical documents.

2

The Bible

The divinity of the Bible can only be proved by the goodness and truth of the Bible. The Bible itself has played a very large part in educating us, and in enabling us to perceive its goodness and truth. Certain utterances, certain statements, are not good and true because they are found in the Bible, but the Bible by including them has been a chief means by which we have gained a knowledge of them, and by which we have, as it were, had our conscience so purified, so moralised, that it can now serve to us as a clearer and surer test than it might have done had there been no Bible to instruct us. Thus the Bible has helped us to prove its own divinity by its own excellence. For divinity means to us eternal righteousness and truth. If you ask me to believe that a book, a law, a saying, is divine, you must ask me to believe that it is divine because it is good and true, and I can only be asked to believe that it is good and true if my conscience, after sifting the matter as best I can, consulting other persons wiser and better than I, and maturely weighing and considering the question all round, allows me to hold and believe that it is good and true. If goodness is the test of divinity, divinity cannot be the test of goodness. And, after all, for us today there is no meaning in divinity except goodness and truth. A bad or false God is a contradiction in terms ...

Now, if this be so, if, namely, the measure of the divinity of the Bible is its measure of goodness and truth and of its influence for goodness and truth, then surely its divineness is very great. But it is not all divine, for it is not all perfectly good, and all perfectly true. There is a lower human element as well as a higher divine element, for though the Bible is all written by men, yet, in the light of what has already been said in this book, it is true to say that its goodness and truth are divine, and that its errors and inadequacies are human. Yet we have always to remember that what may be inadequate for us now and even erroneous, may in its own day have been a moral advance. Hence even in what is now recognised as an error there may be past inspiration.

What we get from examining the Bible itself is what we might expect before we began. For we could not expect to find perfection in any human product. Perfection is the inalienable quality of God, which even He cannot grant to the beings whom He has made. Perfect righteousness, perfect truth, are not capable of being embodied in any book, or of being contained in any single generation or in any human mind. The Divine spirit, as we believe, helps the human spirit in its growth and development. God reveals himself in different degrees to man, but the most inspired writer or speaker is still a man; his inspiration is no guarantee that he will not make mistakes. He will exaggerate; he will err; he will have his national limitations and prejudices. Even in his very conceptions of righteousness he will remain, in many ways, the child of his age. All this we should expect *a priori*, for the Divine cannot be completely contained in the human brain, a human heart, a human will. God cannot make man His secretary or phonograph; in His perfection God remains alone. No human being can be invested with absoluteness. The errors and limitations which we find in every collection of words attributed to a man, however much also attributed to God, are just what we might expect.[1]

THE VALUE OF THE OLD TESTAMENT

The Old Testament, even if we weld its highest conceptions together, and attempt to make of them a consistent and rounded whole, would nevertheless present a religion with many difficulties, some inadequacies and ragged edges. The difficulties we must solve, or leave unsolved, as best we can; the inadequacies we must supply, the ragged edges we must smooth, from other sources. But, even so, it is striking how many fundamental religious conceptions we gain and draw from the Hebrew Bible. There is, for instance, first and foremost the union of religion and morality. People speak, and rightly, of the ethical monotheism of the Prophets. It is that ethical monotheism, with all its difficulties, which is our monotheism today. We cannot learn from the Old Testament what is the origin or explanation of evil. We cannot learn how to combine God's goodness with His omnipotence. The great puzzles are unexplained. But whether in wise or foolish faith, whether as children or as philosophers, whether as saints, or (for the huge majority of us) as very ordinary, average and erring people, who strive to believe in the supremacy of righteousness, we all can draw from the Old Testament our hold upon the divine goodness. That God is good; that goodness, righteousness and love are more inexplicable without Him than with Him, that He is the source of goodness and its cause – these doctrines constitute the kernel of the monotheism today, as they constituted the monotheism of the author of the fifty-first Psalm or the fortieth chapter of Isaiah. Then, again, that we stand in a certain relation to God; that He is our Father and King, our Master and Saviour; this, too, we find in Old Testament religion and this, too, constitutes a large portion of our own. We are His servants and children ordered to obey, but also glad to obey. In obedience are our wisdom and our happiness. And obedience means just that we must try to be good, to execute justice, to love compassion, to walk humbly; to aim at holiness, to 'imitate' the Inimitable, and to love Him. We all admit that such a religion has many difficulties … but in spite of the difficulties, this religion satisfies our reason, our wills and our hearts more than its denial, and more than other religions of which we happen to know.

The outlook of the Old Testament is limited to earth. The doctrine of a life after death, a life not less, but more, worth having than the life on earth, separates both the Rabbinic religion and our own from even the highest 'religion of the Old Testament.' (The few clear allusions to the resurrection in the Old Testament, such as Isaiah 25:19 and Daniel 12:2, can, for my present purpose, be neglected.) But the remarkable point is that though this doctrine makes a great difference, it does not invalidate, it only deepens and spiritualizes, the Old Testament conception of the earthly life. This is a very important matter. The doctrine of the future life does not destroy the value of the earthly life. It does not make it mere preparation. It does not concentrate attention upon earth's sorrow and evils, and regard them as the only fitting occurrences for earthly existence. It does not urge or induce men to think it less important how they fashion and shape their earthly societies. It does not make justice upon earth less desirable because of the higher justice expected in heaven or in the New Jerusalem. It does not suggest that social well-being and happiness and fraternity are either unobtainable or undesirable, or even that it is not our bounden duty to seek for and further them, because a fuller and deeper happiness may await men beyond the grave. The Kingdom of God is still to be realized upon earth, although it is also, or is also to be, realized in heaven. Nay more, the Kingdom of God is progressively realized upon earth, in every piece of righteousness, of love and of unselfish happiness, which we may reciprocally give to, and get from, one another. If 'heaven' is God's world, earth is, or should be made, God's world too; if it is worth while to die for what is to come after death, it is also meant to be worth while to live for what we can and ought to do before we die.

We have deepened the Old Testament view of life, but we have not thrown it over. In this respect Judaism has been consistent throughout the ages. In spite of side-tracks of pessimism and dualism, Judaism has never despaired of earthly life, or disregarded and depressed its value and its happiness. It has always considered it more than a mere stepping-stone to heaven, more than a mere preparation for the life to come. It has never held that earth's sole importance consisted in its being the test of whether you are to spend eternity 'above' or 'below', in misery or in joy.[2]

SOCIAL JUSTICE

It is a weakness of some social philosophies that they confine social ethics to the conduct of individuals in their relations with one another; it is the dangerous fault of other social philosophies that they conceive social ethics wholly in collective terms. It can fairly be said that Jewish ethics, especially in the Bible, combines the two, the social responsibilities of individuals and the collective obligation of society.

The collective obligation of society involves the function of the State and government. The rabbinic view of that function was related to the special position of the Jews in Talmudic times, when there was no Jewish State or government. Jews lived in several countries under non-Jewish rulers. (That occurred even in Biblical times in Babylonia and Egypt.) Neither they, nor others, had the idea that they were an integral part of the peoples among whom they lived; they, because – theoretically at least – they hoped to return to their own land; and others, because they were different in religion, which in the Christian world dominated community life until the modern era. So the Rabbis of the Talmud were mainly concerned with the question of what the Jewish attitude should be to non-Jewish governments. They followed the doctrine, which Jeremiah laid down in his letter to the Jews of Babylonia: 'Seek the peace (i.e., well-being) of the city, and pray to the Lord on its behalf' (Jeremiah 19:7).

During the unrest against Rome before AD 66 a prominent Rabbi urged: 'Pray for the welfare of the government, for if it were not for the fear of it, men would swallow up one another alive.' In the persecution under Hadrian, in the following century, another rabbi declared that in spite of the persecution, the Roman government is entitled to obedience; its dominion must be decreed by Heaven. It is, therefore, a rabbinic principle that 'the law of the country is law'. Government must be obeyed, except when it issues edicts against the Jewish religion. Loyalty to religion is the supreme duty and must be maintained, even if it entails martyrdom, especially if the fundamentals of Judaism are attacked, such as the belief in the One God, the study of the Law, or vital morality. The authority of governments, and the corresponding duty of individuals to obey them, are limited by the demands of religion. In a conflict between them, religion must prevail.

Jeremiah's advice to the exiles in Babylonia ceased to be adequate when, under the influence of political liberalism, Jews were admitted to citizenship in the western world. The change gave them the opportunity and the duty, especially in the democracies, to think out and apply Jewish ideas about the significance of the State and the function of government. For these ideas we have to go back to the Bible, which covers the time when there was a Jewish State.

The first point to note in the Biblical doctrine of government is that the State is conceived as the community – society – organized, with government as its instrument. The idea is nowhere stated explicitly, but it is implied throughout the Bible, in the statements about the Hebrew nation and about the responsibility of kings. The prophets tried to impress on kings the duty to respect the human rights, and to attend to the human needs, of their subjects. With a similar aim, the author of the laws in Deuteronomy prescribes that the king should have by him 'a copy of this law', so that his government may be guided by the principles of righteousness. A psalmist, in a poem (Psalm 72) in honour of a king, prays: 'Give the king thy judgements, O God, and thy righteousness unto the king's son. He shall judge thy people with righteousness, and thy poor with judgement.' The poem in Isaiah 9 describing the ideal king stresses his justice and righteousness. The Messianic prophecies in Isaiah 11 and 32 also ascribe these qualities, in their perfection, to the kings and princes who will rule in the better time to come. Kings were the government of the state. They made, and executed, the edicts which ordered and regulated the life of society. And when the prophets exhort kings to 'do justice and righteousness, deliver the despoiled from the hands of the oppressor, commit no wrong or violence against the stranger, the orphan and the widow', in short, 'to defend the cause of the poor and needy' (Jeremiah 22:3 and 16), they meant that it was the king's duty to protect the weak members of society from oppression by the strong. But the oppression was not always merely (though that was bad enough) the arbitrary exercise of power, whether the power of office or the power of wealth; it also resulted from laws that weighed heavily on the poor – laws, for example, that gave a rich creditor the legal right to take the field of a poor farmer who could not pay a debt.

It may all be fairly translated into: It is the duty of government to maintain justice in its laws and in its law courts, and its laws must aim to establish a social order which respects human persons and cares for human lives. There is a hint of this positive social duty of government in the Rabbinic saying that it is the function of government to keep the stronger from swallowing up the weaker, the function, that is, to protect the weak. The community was conceived as an organic unit, with the collective responsibility to protect and help its weaker members, by ordering its corporate life according to justice and love, so as to be a society infused with righteousness ...

The obedience which the individual owes to government is

another part of the duty which individuals owe to society. There is no law in the Bible commanding that obedience, nor do the prophets exhort to it. When the Hebrews were a nation, it was just assumed; though the prophets at times refused to give it, out of obedience to the dictates of their conscience. But generally, the conception of government as the representative of the community entitles it to authority over individuals. But it is not unlimited authority. Far from it. For government, as the instrument of society, must fulfil the collective obligation of society to respect the rights of individuals. The principle may be put differently. Government is entitled to obedience when it obeys the moral law. In this way, the authority of the State and the freedom of the individual are harmonized.

The principle that government is subject to moral law is enunciated by the prophets in their sermons to kings and nations. They would have been roused to passionate indignation by Machiavelli's view that 'it must be understood that a prince, and especially a new prince, cannot observe all those things which are considered good in men, being often obliged in order to maintain the State to act against faith, against charity, against humanity and against religion'.

The Machiavellian idea has been followed – all too faithfully – by dictators in all ages. The prophets would have condemned, with equal vehemence, the idea that a nation's foreign policy should be guided by criteria of power or profit without regard for moral principles. Against such doctrines, and policies, the prophets thundered. It is the duty of the king 'to do justice and righteousness', and the law-giver enjoined kings to follow the moral law, the law of God.[3]

OLD TESTAMENT DEFICIENCIES?

Does the Old Testament, at its very highest, leave any religious gaps and deficiencies? Are there, in other words, any rough edges in the Old Testament to the smoothing of which the Old Testament itself makes of itself no contribution whatever? I think the answer must be that there are remarkably few. It may be that the higher doctrine and the complementary conception is only very occasionally taught; it may be that we can only cite as examples one or two brief passages, incidental and disconnected.

Nevertheless, an indication, a suggestion, often, indeed, a definite, if isolated statement, are there. That is why, I suppose, Jews are usually so emphatic that, possessing the Old Testament, they have nothing to learn from the New. It is not merely prejudice. It is not merely a wilful shutting of the eyes. It is also something more and better. It is that they are so familiar with these incidental and occasional utterances of the Old Testament that they regard them as its dominant and prevailing view. They get everything they can get out of the few sentences which teach the doctrine they desire and cherish; they squeeze out of them all that can possibly be extracted, and perhaps a little more! They ignore the many, or the prevailing, passages which could be quoted on the other side. As an estimate of the Old Testament as a whole this Jewish attitude towards it is unscientific and inaccurate. Nevertheless these occasional and exceptional passages are in the book; they do form part of it. If attention is concentrated upon them, if what is in conflict with them is neglected (or explained away), then it is not unreasonable, and it is certainly not surprising, that men should repudiate the view that for the source, or for an exposition, of the doctrines these passages contain, it is necessary to go beyond the pages of the Old Testament. And it is true that there is much more filling out to be found in the New Testament than actual or entire novelty. The rough edges of the Old Testament are smoothed, its gaps and deficiencies are, for the most part, filled up, by the Old Testament itself. It is its own correction and supplement. What the New Testament does is to correct and supplement afresh, sometimes more fully, sometimes more brilliantly, sometimes with fresh illumination and from a novel point of view. Or again, as we have seen, it develops a doctrine and pushes it towards its logical end. But it does not, for the most part, contain what we, from our Liberal Jewish point of view, can regard as completely new doctrine which is also true doctrine. And of those few Old Testament edges which are rough, and which the Old Testament itself makes no incidental and occasional attempt at smoothing, the New Testament smoothes by no means all. Some it leaves untouched, no less rough than it found them.[4]

THE PROPHETS

It was the prophets, men few in number, but great in power, who gave to the religion of Israel its specific character and direction. The seed was sown by Moses, the Founder; the ground was watered by Samuel, by Nathan and Gad, by Elijah and Micah; but the harvest was gathered, or rather it was ripened, by the prophets of the eighth century. It was they who definitely connected the worship of Yahweh with the practice of morality, and conceived the idea of a holy nation, divinely chosen and divinely trained. They were the first to show how the triumph of a nation's God – his veritable 'day' of glory – might be signalized by his people's punishment and defeat. It was the prophets who purified the conception of Yahweh as a God of righteousness and naught besides, and began the transformation of the only God of a single nation into the only God of the entire world. And, lastly, it was the prophets of the eighth century who began to teach the doctrine – so strange to antiquity – that a single God of one people might become the One God of all. Thus the prophets point forward on the one hand to the Law, which sought by definite enactment and discipline to help on the schooling of the holy nation, living apart and consecrated to God, and on the other hand to the Apostle of Tarsus, who carried the universalist idea to its final and practical conclusion.

It was inevitable that the prophets should leave some room for future development. Their teaching contained the seeds of many subsequent antinomies. Their attitude towards the outward embodiment of religion was left vague and undefined. They had attacked the cultus, but they had suggested nothing in its place; they had inveighed against forms, but they had not given the people any vehicle of ceremonial expression for religious life: they had only said, 'seek God, seek goodness', counsels too elevated or too abstract for their generation to apply. Moreover, in spite of their denunciation of present abuses, they had been all too optimistic as to the not too distant future. They had threatened a sinful society with summary punishment; but, anticipating a speedy recovery from disaster, they had predicted a renovated community, chastened by suffering and purged of guilt. They contracted the progressive drama of history into a single scene. All kinds of puzzling problems arose out of their teaching. The punishment and the deliverance came, but the Messianic age did not follow. Was sin still uneradicated, or were the children suffering for the iniquities of their fathers? Again, the prophetical unit was the nation and not the individual, and national well-being was characterised in outward and material terms. Sin brought adversity, but reform and penitence would bring welfare and content. Prosperity was the test of goodness and its reward. Even for nations this doctrine has its dangers; apply it, as later teachers did, to the individual, and you find yourself hopelessly at variance with fact. And lastly, although the prophets began to emancipate the religion of Israel from its tribalism – to turn Yahweh into God – they helped at the same time to produce a particularism narrower and more fatal than that which they had destroyed. For Yahweh, though the only God, remained the God of Israel, and the nations were not solely regarded as independent creations of the One Creator – ends in themselves, as we should now say – but also, and sometimes mainly, as instruments to promote God's purposes in the training of his chosen people. For as Wellhausen has finely said, 'the present which was passing before the prophets became to them, as it were, the plot of a divine drama which they watched with an intelligence that anticipated the denouement. Everywhere the same goal of development, everywhere the same laws. The nations are the *dramatis personae*, Israel the hero, Yahweh the author of the tragedy.' But in this tragedy of which Israel is the hero, the nations only too readily assumed the villain's part. The eighth-century prophets did not yet so characterise the players, and the universalism of Isaiah enabled him to change Assyria, the rod of Yahweh's anger, into Assyria, the work of Yahweh's hands. But already in Ezekiel the nations are naturally and essentially the wicked enemies of Israel and God, and the same identification was repeated again and again, though not without excuse, by subsequent writers after the captivity in Babylon. This, as we shall see, was the problem which the Judaism of Ezra and his successors, in spite of a never forgotten and never renounced idea of universalism, failed to solve. Only Modern Judaism, upon the moral side at least, has effected a solution.

But these blemishes and imperfections of their teaching were as nothing to the greatness of the work which was accomplished by the prophets for their own age and for posterity.

Parallels to many of their noblest sayings can pretty easily be collected from other religious literatures both of the East and of the West. Deeper appreciation and fuller discussion of the dark problems of human destiny are to be found among the thinkers of India, and, here and there, among the thinkers of Greece. Ignorant as the prophets were of any bodily resurrection upon earth, still more of any spiritual life beyond the grave, a whole province of religious aspiration was cut off from them; and with that loss, the light which such beliefs alone can shed upon many important questions, such as sin and retribution, the transfiguration which they alone can effect upon the conception of earthly joys and earthly sorrows, could not be seen or anticipated. The very manner and occasion of their utterance are partly cause and partly result of the complete lack in all the prophetic writings of that mystic element in religion which hovers between the highest truth and the wildest. But no other teaching of the ancient world can show a similar grasp upon the essentials of true religion.[5]

THE LEGALISM OF THE OLD TESTAMENT

There would seem to have been a legal element in Judaism from the beginning, just as there was from the beginning, and always, something more than legalism – other elements besides the legal element. Tradition makes Moses both Prophet and Lawgiver. It did not seem absurd to the tradition to think of him as combining functions which we are wont to think of as distinct, or even as antagonistic. It could even think of him as Priest, a function which we, I think, combine more easily with the Lawgiver than with the Prophet. It is also noteworthy that biblical Hebrew has no word which exactly translates our word Law. The Ten Commandments are called the Ten Words, or Sayings. 'Remember the Torah of Moses my Servant', and Torah is not quite rightly translated by Law. Teaching of which ordinances form a part, and from which ordinances and rules of conduct and practice may be deduced, seems to be the meaning of the word which soon predominated. The Rabbis declared that the Prophets were Torah, the Psalms were Torah; indeed the whole Bible was Torah.

Yet, though there were Laws and ordinances from the days

of the Founder onwards – many of which, it may be presumed, have perished – the gradual writing of them down, the gradual general acknowledgement of them as the ordinances of God, the gradual attribution of them all to the Founder, and the gradual acceptance of that strange, unhistoric attribution, till it became a fixed and fundamental dogma of the Faith – all this, together with the welding together of those various codes and accretion to codes into one 'book', the text of which was long before fixed and unalterable, whether for addition or diminution, constituted events of enormous importance and influence in the history and development of Judaism: Judaism created the Pentateuch, but it is, nevertheless, largely true to say that, in the form which Judaism assumed for some two thousand years, the Pentateuch created Judaism.

The legalism of Judaism must, therefore, be acknowledged. It must be emphasised neither too little nor too much. The Pentateuch became the most important portion of the O.T., and perhaps the unsystematic nature of Judaism, its varying tones, its manifold aspects, may be due to the fact that the sacred writings on which it rests are not the 'five books of Moses', but the strange medley of documents which form the O.T.

To the men who formed the Judaism that has continued from their day to this – I mean the Rabbis and Teachers of the couple of centuries, shall we say, before Christ and of a couple of centuries after him – it was no inconsistency to use the Prophets to back up the Pentateuch, and the Pentateuch to back up the Prophets. The Rabbis of the Talmudic ages, at all events, seem to have known the whole O.T. by heart, and they freely quote from every part of it. Hence their legalism (as Jewish scholars have often pointed out) is not precisely the legalism which the non-Jewish community supposes it to be. It has, indeed, the characteristics of the conventional legalism, of the conventional legal religion, and is liable to some of the faults usually attributed to that legalism. To that extent, the Pentateuch, and the O.T. as containing the Pentateuch, are responsible for the existence of these faults. But the odd thing is that the O.T. is also responsible (by reason of its variety) for the excellences of Jewish legalism, for its peculiar character, which made it so different from the legalism of modern convention, which caused it, as it were, to include the corrections to its own weaknesses. To every Christian generation since Paul legalism has had something of the evils and the weaknesses which this singular genius found in the religion he abandoned. But every Jewish generation since Paul (though some more than others) found in it the road to God instead of the road to sin, the means of overcoming temptation instead of the cause of it, the source of joy and freedom instead of the source of anguish and slavery. So strange is that Jewish legalism which the O.T. contributed to produce.[6]

NOTES

1. Claude Montefiore, *Outlines of Liberal Judaism*, London: Macmillan (1912).
2. Claude Montefiore, *Liberal Judaism and Hellenism*, London: Macmillan (1918), pp. 20–3.
3. Israel Mattuck, *Jewish Ethics*, London: Hutchinson (1953), pp. 83–7.
4. Claude Montefiore, *The Old Testament and After*, London: Macmillan (1923), pp. 285–8.
5. Claude Montefiore, *The Hibbert Lectures on the Origin and Growth of Religion as Illustrated by the Ancient Hebrews*, London: Williams and Norgate (1892), pp. 156–9.
6. Claude Montefiore, 'The Old Testament and Judaism', in H. Wheeler-Robinson (ed.), *Record and Revelation*, Oxford: The Clarendon Press (1938), pp. 11–14.

3

Christianity and the New Testament

In the greatest gifts of God to struggling humanity there seems to be a double strand. Even in the Hebrew Bible, for example, we found doctrines which we could not regard as good and true, and we found them mixed up and blended with, and even sustaining and assisting, doctrines which seemed to us wholly right and pure. The world seems to be carried forward by new good which is not yet wholly good, or which yet contains within it seeds of evil. It is taught and helped by fresh truths, which contain within them germs of falsehood. Great and noble results are often achieved through illusion and error: few recognise the illusion till the results are secured ...

To my mind, and to the mind of most Jews, this mixture of truth and falsehood is curiously illustrated by the religious teaching of the 'New Testament'. There is much in that book which is great and noble, much which is sublime and tender, much which is good and true. Of this 'much', the greater consists in a fresh presentment of some of the best and highest teaching in the 'Old Testament', in a vivid reformulation of it, in an admirable picking and choosing, an excellent bringing together. But a part consists of a further development, or in a clear or more emphatic expression of certain truths which previously were only implicit or not fully drawn out. Thus of its excellence part may in this sense be called old, and part in this sense may be called new. But in close and curious combination with what is good there are some things which are erroneous and harmful, and there are others which are liable to dangerous perversion, or which hold within them germs of evil and have borne evil fruit ...

For good and for evil – and the two have been strangely inter-woven together – the New Testament has been of enormous influence in the moral and religious history of the world. For that reason alone all Jews who, like other civilised persons, want to know about that history must read the New Testament, and read it, if they can, with impartial minds, ready to receive the good and to reject the evil. But it cannot be admitted into a Jewish Bible for Home Reading. Not only that the critical study of it is unsuited for the young. There is more than this involved. For if it be said that within the Hebrew Bible too we have found higher and lower teaching, doctrine to reject as well as doctrine to receive, this argument would not suffice for the inclusion of the New Testament into the Bible of the Jews. It is one thing to observe, with growing thought and developing conceptions of religion and morality, deficiencies and unevenness in the sacred scriptures which have been your community's sacred scriptures for 2000 years; it is quite another thing to add on to those scriptures other writings in which evils and errors, some of them which I have mentioned above, are known and recog-nised to exist. Moreover, the grave errors, which we Jews think that we can detect in the New Testament, are very closely connected with, even if they do not actually constitute, its most essential teachings. These errors are in fact among the very points, which the great mass of Christians regard as its most peculiar characteristics and its most vital truths. Some of them, at any rate, seem to us to contradict the teaching of the Old Testament just where that teaching is at its truest, its purest and its best. For these reasons, even if there were no others, the Bible of the Jews must remain limited to the books, which now compose it.[1]

JESUS THE JEW

What do we really know of the life of the man who is said to have lived the most perfect and adorable life that ever was lived? Nothing more, practically, than what we are told in the Gospel of Mark. And how fragmentary, how small this is. In all probability all that we are told about him relates to one single year of his life – the last. And of this one year, how much do we really know? How many incidents are related of it? How many of these incidents are above suspicion, and how many of them are of a kind in which high nobility of character is revealed? Very few.

In all probability the life of a peripatetic Jewish teacher of the first century was not one of peculiar hardship. In spite of a certain famous verse in Matthew, there is no good evidence that, for the greater part of his teaching career, Jesus had any gigantic troubles and difficulties to encounter or grave sacrifices to make. Then we come to the journey to Jerusalem, the last days and the death. And here, too, uncertainty dogs us still. We cannot tell for sure whether Jesus went to Jerusalem with the expectation of life and revealed Messiahship or with the expectation of death. But, in spite of the famous cry upon the cross, which can either be explained away or regarded as unauthentic, let us suppose that he went prepared for death. It is quite as probable as, if not more probable than, the contrary hypothesis. Who shall then deny the nobility of his action, the beauty and the greatness of his sacrifice?

But the outsider is compelled to declare that, even so, we do not know enough of Jesus – the records are too small and too uncertain – for us to assert categorically that this man's life was unique, perfect and unapproachable. The material shrinks together. We may, if we please, call the ideal life – and each of us will make up his own ideal – the life of Christ. But to call the life of the historic Jesus the flawless exemplar, the essence, the completion, the fullness, of the absolutely perfect life, seems to me exaggerated and impossible. It is not so much that there are one or two holes to pick in what we know. It is not that there are a few easy (Christians would say shallow) criticisms to make in this action of his or in that. It is that what we do know (if 'know' be indeed the word) is so extremely small. An heroic death, upon the one interpretation, is undoubted. But can we speak of an heroic life? Where are the noble deeds? We cannot make a list of them, for they simply do not exist.

Nevertheless, through the mist and the uncertainty and the paucity of the evidence, we seem to see the lineaments of a striking, character. We seem to see a man aflame with love of God and love of man, who passed his short life, and encountered his awful death, in their true and unflagging service. We seem to see a man of singular purity of soul, and of absolute sincerity of purpose. A large-hearted man, who gazed into the deepest nature of righteousness, and realized the very essence of true religion. A man who loved and was beloved, who looked below the surface, and could recognize the germs of goodness beneath neglect and ignorance and sin. A hater of shams and hypocrisy and formalism and conceit, yet, withal, a man conscious of his own power, his own inspiration, his own message and mission from God. A man of great tenderness, of deep compassion, he cared deeply for the waifs and strays, the flotsam and jetsam, of humanity, who were often more sinned against than sinning. Yet a strong man too, and fearless, who could denounce those from whom he differed, those who opposed his teaching, and those in whom he saw, or thought he saw, the sins he specially hated – self-righteousness, hypocrisy, formalism – with the utmost force, and with, perhaps, exaggerated violence. A lover of children, and a lover of nature, simple, serene and single-eyed; no ascetic, no solitary, but independent of material needs, detached, because his higher duty, as he believed, demanded it, from all human ties of family or state. He lived for his fellow Jews and died for them: he lived in obedience to his mission, and in intimate communion with God. A holy man, undoubtedly; one who realized the Fatherhood of God with vivid intensity, and lived habitually as in His presence.

Such, apparently, was Jesus. Not perfect, not sinless, but a striking personality, who left the deepest impression upon his followers. Not for the adherents of Liberal Judaism the one and only Master, not the adored exemplar of all perfection, not the One Consummate Teacher, whose words must not be criticised, subtracted from, or added to, but yet for all time, and without question, a noble and illustrious Jew ...

To develop seems easier than to lay the broad foundations. We will not minimise the greatness of the New Testament, or cheapen the originality whether of Jesus or Paul. But when we compare the achievement of the Old Testament with that of the New, we realise how much greater is our obligation to the Old. When you have won through to your monotheism, and to the doctrine of the One Good God, when you have got your prophets with their weaving together of religion and morality, when you have got your commands and ideals to love God with all your heart, and the neighbour and resident alien as yourself, when you have reached the ideals of justice and compassion, of the clean hands and the pure heart – why, then, it was, in a sense, comparatively easy to supplement, to bring together, to purify, to universalise. Only comparatively easy, of course! The achievements of Jesus and Paul (in spite of some sad retrogressions) are great achievements. But what we owe to them seems but little in comparison with what we owe to their Old Testament predecessors. The bulk of our religion and the bulk of our morality seem due neither to Jesus nor to Paul, neither to Plato nor to Epictetus, but to the Sacred Scripture of the Jews. For Liberal Jews and Liberal Judaism, the Old Testament remains primary and fundamental, the New Testament secondary and supplemental ... the supplementary and complementary teachings in the New Testament we will also make use of and frankly admire, but the Old Testament, both in regard to what it says and to what it does not say, to what it contains and what it omits, abides as the basis of our faith, as our stronghold and our charter.[2]

JEWS AND THE NEW TESTAMENT

It might be asked: what is, or what should be, the Jewish interest in the New Testament, in the Synoptic Gospels, or in the life and character of Jesus? ... The origin of a great religion, which filled so immense a place in the history of the world, must surely be of interest to every cultivated person. To know something about a Book and a Person that have been of such huge and amazing importance, and that are of such great importance still, is a right and reasonable thing – a desirable part of knowledge. But the European Jew lives in a Christian environment, a Christian civilisation. He has absorbed much of this civilisation himself; he breathes in it; it is part of him. He reads the history of the country of which he is the citizen. This civilisation and this country are unintelligible without Christianity. They rest upon the New Testament and the Gospels. The book, which has had the greatest influence upon European history and European civilization, is the Bible. The Jew does not mind saying and repeating this. But he too often forgets that the Bible that has had this influence is not merely the Old Testament. It is the Old Testament and the New Testament combined. And of the two, it is the New Testament, which has undoubtedly had the greater influence and has been of greater importance. It is the Gospels and the life of Christ, which have most markedly determined European history and has most influenced for good or evil many millions of lives. If it is an improper ignorance not to have read some portions of Shakespeare or Milton, it is, I am inclined to think, a much more improper ignorance not to have read the Gospels.

The curiosity of the Jew as regards these writings might also be legitimately aroused when he reflects that the Gospel hero was a Jew, and that the books of the New Testament were mainly written by Jews. Jewish ignorance of the New Testament is indeed not unnatural. It has many causes, which I will not here enumerate. It needs, even today perhaps, some detachment of mind to say: 'I will read and study the book upon which is based the religion which has inflicted upon my ancestors such incalculable cruelty and wrong. I will read and study the book from which comes the religion which vaunts itself to be a religion of love, but which, so far as my race is concerned, has usually been a religion of hate. I will read and study the book from which proceeds a monotheism, less pure and lofty than my own, a monotheism, if it can be called such, which has deified a man and invented the Trinity. I will read and study the book from which was evolved the religion which pretends to have superseded and to be superior to my own – to be purer and better than my religion, of which the cardinal doctrines are contained in such words as: "Hear, O Israel, The Lord thy God, the Lord is One. They shalt love thy neighbour as thyself. What does the Lord require of thee, but to do justly, and to love mercy, and to walk humbly with thy God?"'

Yet this detachment of mind must now be demanded. Judaism, and therefore the Jews or some Jews, must answer the questions, and answer them better and more impartially than they have yet been faced and answered: what is the right Jewish attitude towards the New Testament? What are we to think about the Gospels and the Gospels' hero? I cannot believe that the best and final answers will be purely negative. They will not be formed along the familiar lines that what is new in the Gospels is not true, and what is true is not new.

Does Judaism really expect that in the future – even the distant future – the Old Testament will be 'accepted' and the New Testament 'rejected'? Does Judaism really expect that the Bible, for the Europe of the 'Messianic' age, will be a smaller Bible than the European Bible today? Will it include the Old Testament only? But if such an idea is inconceivable, if the Bible for Europe has been constituted once and for all – whatever men may think of its theologies – should not Judaism take up some more reasoned and studied attitude towards so permanent a part of the religious literature and religious consciousness of the Western world?

One view which will be incidentally maintained and supported in this commentary is that Judaism has something to gain and absorb from the New Testament. There are teachings in the New Testament, and above all in the Gospels, which supplement and carry forward some essential teachings in the Old Testament. It seems true to say that in respect of moral and religious value we can dispense neither with the Old Testament nor with the New Testament. I will not attempt to sum up here the special excellences and values of either. So far as the Gospels are concerned, these excellences will be alluded to in the commentary. But over and above the excellences in detail, there is the spirit or impression of the whole. So too with the Old Testament, the Hebrew Bible. The strong, virile, healthy tone of the Old Testament religious teaching is sometimes contrasted with a certain sentimentality and introspectiveness in the New. Its vigorous social and 'collective' morality – its insistence upon justice and, righteousness in society and the state – are also sometimes contrasted with a certain marked individualism in the New. Contrasts proverbially exaggerate, yet there may be something not wholly false in this contrast as in others. Meanwhile we need both the Old Testament's imperative demand for a righteous nation, and the New Testament's insistent emphasis upon the value of the individual soul; we need both the severity of justice and the tenderness of love. As regards the latter pair of apparent opposites they are both present in both Testaments, but in different ways. And these different ways could themselves be made to form one illustration the more for my contention that an Englishman, a German, or a Frenchman, be he Christian or be he Jew, has something to gain, something of moral or religious value to absorb, both from the New Testament and the Old, or, if the collocation be more emphatic, both from the Gospel and the Law.[3]

A JEWISH STUDY OF JESUS

For Jews – so long as they are and remain Jews (i.e. members of the Jewish faith) – the great interest or value of the Synoptic Gospels lies in the teaching of Jesus rather than in his personality or the life. We persist in separating the one from the other, whereas to Christians they form a unity, a whole. From his childhood upwards the Jew's highest conceptions of goodness and God have never been associated with Jesus. These conceptions may have been due to an idealisation of O.T. teaching or Rabbinic teaching or both. Some might argue (whether wrongly or rightly) that they are partly due to a conscious absorption and adoption of Christian and Gospel teaching. But, consciously and deliberately, his highest conceptions of goodness and God have been ever presented to the Jew, whether the orthodox or liberal Jew, as wholly, and characteristically Jewish. Moreover, he has it ingrained into him that there need and can be nothing – no mediator, no divine man – between himself and God. The position of Jesus, the place he fills, even in Unitarian Christianity, is impossible for the Jew, for two reasons which, at first sight, may seem somewhat irreconcilable with each other. God is too 'far'; God is too 'near'. To make Jesus as 'divine' as Christians make him seems to the Jew presumptuous and out of the question. Man is man, he says; God is God. The best man is infinitely removed from the perfect goodness of God, and the fullness of the divine righteousness can be revealed in no man's life. On the other hand, God is so near that there is no room, as well as no need, for a *tertium quid* between man and God. The Jew, so long as he is and remains a Jew, simply cannot believe that any man was ever endowed with the fullness of every conceivable moral excellence – that any man was ever wholly sinless, and conscious of his sinlessness, the more perfect because of this consciousness, the acme and cream of goodness and love. The Jew simply cannot believe in such a being, on the one hand, and he has no room or place for him on the other. Jesus has not introduced the Jews to God in their childhood; they do not require him in order to get to God in their manhood.

But the teaching of Jesus abides. The unprejudiced Jew, even remaining a Jew, can find bits of his teaching which go beyond O.T. teaching, or which at any rate bring out occasional

utterances and teachings of the O.T. more clearly and fully. Jesus
links on to the Prophets, and sometimes seems to go beyond
them. Let us imagine that the writings of a new Hebrew Prophet,
a contemporary of, say, Isaiah or Jeremiah, were brought to
light. The Jewish position would not be changed but the Jews
would be delighted to obtain some fresh teachings and sayings
of beauty and value, and even of originality, to add to those
which they already possess. So it is, or so it can be, as regards
Jesus and the Gospel. But the Christian, even the Unitarian
Christian, has received the highest conceptions of God and
righteousness through Jesus. To the Christian, alike in his teaching and in his personality and life, Jesus reveals God. To the
Christian, even to the Unitarian Christian, the N.T. is the book
which tells him most truly and fully about goodness and God,
and within the N.T. it is the Gospels which tell him best of all.
He fits in Jesus with his purest thoughts of God; Jesus brings
God near to him. Whereas to the Jews, Jesus – or any man –
would be in their way in their relations with, and in their
approaches to, God, to the Christian, even to the Unitarian
Christian Jesus smoothes the way to God and shortens it. He
is the way. Without Jesus – if that fatality could for a moment
be conceived – God, even to the Unitarian Christian, would be
more distant and more dim; without Jesus, God, to the Jew,
would be no less near and no less bright.

Again, the value of the teaching in the Synoptic Gospels does
not really depend on whether it was said by Jesus or not. No
doubt, if you could *prove* that Peter told Mark in Aramaic every
word of chapter vii, and that Mark wrote it all down in Greek,
the likelihood that Mark 7:14[4] was actually said by Jesus would
be immensely increased. But the value or the truth of the saying
would not be increased. It would remain as before. The magni-
ficence of the teaching in Matt. 25:40[5] remains the same whether
Jesus said it or did not; the hatefulness of the teaching in Matt.
25:33, 41, 46[6] remains the same likewise. Moreover, in any case,
Jesus gave the impetus for the teaching of the Gospel as a whole.
It can now be *regarded* as a whole and assessed as a whole. We
can just speak of its aroma, its spirit, whether Jesus said everything which is ascribed to him or not.

And there is something more. The exact truth, or exact
measure of truth, in the stories about the life and death of Jesus
does not, from one point of view, matter so much to us, or affect

us so much, as it would have affected our ancestors. To them, whether Jew or Christian, it was often a question of *all* true or *all* false. To us there are degrees, and even kinds, of truth.[7]

THE GOOD SAMARITAN

Whether or not the Good Samaritan was originally a Midrashic illustration of Leviticus 19:18,[8] its effectiveness for that end is, as the Parable now stands, indisputable. In Mr Montefiore's admirable words the parable [is] 'one of the simplest and noblest among the noble gallery of parables in the Synoptic Gospels. Love, it tells us, must know no limits of race and ask no enquiry. Who needs me is my neighbour. Whom at the given time and place I can help with my active love, he is my neighbour and I am his.' Curiously enough, it is the heirs of the Pharisees who most strenuously insist on this ...

Attention may be drawn in this context to a remarkable passage in the Sifra. Here the collocation 'Priest, Levite, Israelite' is referred to in terms which for their universal sympathy are worthy to be placed side by side with the moral of the Parable of the Good Samaritan. The text, Leviticus 18:5, runs thus: 'Ye shall keep My statutes and My ordinances, which, if a man do, he shall live in (or by) them: I am the Lord.' Whereon the Sifra has this comment:

> *Which, if a man do.* Rabbi Jeremiah was wont to say: Whence does one infer that even a heathen who performs the Law is accounted as a High Priest? The text proves this, when it says, 'which, if a *man* do, he shall live by them.' Similarly, the Scripture says: 'This is the law' – it does not say 'This is the law of Priests, Levites, and Israel,' but 'This is the law of *man*, O Lord God' (2 Sam.7: 19). Thus also the text does not say 'Open ye the gates that Priests, Levites and Israelites may enter,' but 'Open ye the gates, that *the righteous heathen* which keepeth truth (or faithfulness) may enter in' (Isaiah 16:2). Similarly the Psalmist (118:21) does not say: 'This is the gate of the Lord; Priests, Levites, and Israelites shall enter into it,' but, 'This is the gate of the Lord; the *righteous* shall enter into it.' So, too, with Ps 33:1, the call is not to Priests, Levites and Israelites, but to *the*

righteous to rejoice in the Lord. Nor does the text (Ps.125:4) say: 'Do good, O Lord, unto Priests, Levites and Israelites,' but 'Do good, O Lord, unto those that be good, and to them that are upright in their hearts.' Hence even a heathen who performs the law is accounted as a High Priest.

Nowhere can contrast be more easily discerned between Paulinism and Pharisaism than in the respective uses made of the ground text (Leviticus 18:5) on which this remarkable homily is based. Paul quotes the text twice (Romans 10:5 and Galatians 3:12). To him, the abrogation of the Law makes it possible for all men to be one in Christ (Gal. 3:23–28). To the Pharisee, all men may become one in and because of the Law. To Paul the collocation Jew, male, freeman was objectionable; to the Pharisee the collocation Priest, Levite, Israelite. Both Paul and the Pharisee would embrace all mankind in the one gracious possibility of divine love.

The appearance of the Samaritan among the personages of the Parable is explicable, not only on such general grounds, but also as a device of moral art. To castigate one's own community, it is sometimes effective to praise those outside it. We have a very early instance of it in the Talmud. The traditions of it are many; it clearly emanates from an age when the Temple still stood. The hero of the story is Dama, son of Netinah. He was a non-Jew, an idolator, dwelling in Askelon; evidently a man of means ... 'To what limits should a son go in honouring his father?' asked the Rabbi. 'Go forth and see what a certain idolator of Askelon did' is the answer. On one occasion he was silent and respectful when his mother publicly insulted him, and on another occasion refused to disturb his father, who lay asleep with his head on the key of the box containing the gem which the agents of the Sanhedrin wished to purchase for the High Priest's vestment. Though a very high price was offered, he refused to disturb his father, and the sale was not effected. In this way, a heathen was put forward as the model of love and reverence towards parents. This is a Pharisaic parallel to the choice of a Samaritan in the Lucan Parable. The parallel is even closer when Luke quotes Jesus as pointing to a Samaritan as a 'stranger' as the only one out of ten cleansed lepers who 'returned to give glory to God' (Luke 17:16). As J. A. Montgomery aptly remarks, 'The gratitude of the Samaritan was

made to point a moral to the Jews even as was the faith of a
heathen centurion upon another occasion (Matthew 8:5 ff.).'

All art, even the highest, is necessarily imperfect, and so fine
an example of the Parabolic art as the Good Samaritan does not
escape the universal condition. In order to include the moral
becomes exclusive; to bring the Samaritan into the category of
'neighbour', the Priest and Levite are excluded. Julicher asks
these questions with much force, and concludes that verses
30–35 belong to a different context in which the question related
not to the definition of 'neighbour', but to the qualifications for
admission to the Kingdom. The merciful alien better deserves
admission than the Jewish Temple official enslaved to selfish-
ness. (Cf. Romans 2:14 ff.) By this means, however, the situation
is not saved. For we are again, indeed, faced by the real paradox
in the Gospel criticism of the Pharisees; it excludes *them* from
the gracious message which Jesus brought. This, as Julicher
argues, is not a forward step, but a step backward from Pharisaic doctrine. That by Priest and Levite are meant the Pharisaic
leaders cannot be seriously questioned. John (1:19) preserves a
true tradition of this method of classifying the official representatives of Judaism, and it is not without significance that while
the Synoptists generally use the dichotomy Pharisees and Scribes,
we have in the chapter of Luke under discussion the Johannine
division. And there is this difference between the Lucan parable
and the Rabbinic use of a non-Jew as model. The Rabbis do not
forget that their own class is capable of the same virtue …

It is indeed remarkable how many stories are to be found in
the Rabbinic sources of conduct very like that of the Good
Samaritan. A series of anecdotes at the end of Tractate Peah in
the Jerusalem Talmud show how keenly the Pharisees felt it
their duty to relieve distress on their way, even when their
benevolence was being exploited by impostors. The story of
Abba Talna has already been told above; how at the anticipated
sacrifice of all his goods he carried to the city a leper whom he
found by the way-side. Nahum of Gimzu acted less promptly,
but the sharpness of his remorse and the severity of the retribution that met him are full of significance. Carrying a gift to
his father-in-law, he was accosted by a leper who begged alms.
'On my way back,' answered Nahum. On his return he found
the leper dead. He exclaimed: 'May my eyes which saw you
and gave not be blinded! My hands that stretched not out be

cut off, my legs that ran not to thee be broken!' And so it happened to him. To R. Aqiba he declared: 'My remorse is great, and my sufferings are the just requital of my wrong towards this poor fellow.'[9]

DID JESUS INTEND TO FOUND A NEW RELIGION?

If we ask wherein his hearers found the teachings of Jesus 'new, inspired, prophetic ...' it is not quite easy to reply. For, except as regards the Law, one can probably discover parallels in the Rabbinic literature to every portion of his teaching. But the words 'new, inspired, prophetic' are nevertheless not rashly nor falsely chosen. It is the spirit of the teaching, its unity, its fervour, its intensity, its enthusiasm, which were new, inspired, prophetic, rather than any one particular part of it. Pity, faith, love, trust – contemporary Rabbis spoke of all these things, but they did not, perhaps, speak of them with the same intensity and genius. They did not, perhaps, quite in the same way, demand all for the Highest. They did not preach the same impassioned doctrine of sacrifices. They did not show the same yearning to save the sinner from the fastnesses and morasses of sin or from the physical or mental evils which in those days were so closely associated with sin. It was in these more indefinable and subtler ways that the teaching, like the bearing, of Jesus was new, inspired, prophetic, rather then in any novelty of doctrine in any one definite particular.

The important points in which the teaching of Jesus was opposed to the Rabbis are all connected with the Law. His teaching about divorce, about the Sabbath, about clean and unclean, was in the spirit of the prophets, but not in strict accordance with the letter of the Law. His conflict with Rabbis did not come because he went beyond their teaching about loving one's enemies, or about the deep value of inward purity in itself, or of every sort of inwardness itself; the conflict came because Jesus drew certain practical conclusions in respect to Inwardness and these conclusions led logically to a transgression of the Law. The doctrine of the divine Law put both ceremonial and moral injunctions on an equal footing, and never contemplated any conflict between them. It gave no clear guide for action should such a conflict ever arise. This doctrine of the divine law, with divinity extending to the ceremonial as well as to the moral, placed both Jesus and the Rabbis in a very difficult position. For Jesus, too, though less fervently than his Rabbinical opponents, professed to believe, and did actually believe, in the divineness of the law. But his impassioned prophetic attitude drove him on to action and teaching which were in violation of the Law, while the Rabbis, in their profound veneration and adoration of the God-given and perfect Law, could not look at the relation of morality to ceremonial, of the Inward to the Outward, from a purely prophetic point of view. The conflict between Jesus and the Rabbis was thus inevitable and had all the elements of tragedy. It was 'tragic' and produced a tragedy.

Another gravely important question which may be asked about the teaching of Jesus is: did he intend to found a new religion? This question is distinct from the other one as to whether his teaching is sufficiently novel, distinctive, and comprehensive as to justify a separate religion with a separate name being founded upon it, even apart from any doctrine as to his Messiahship or divinity. Such might be the position of much modern Unitarianism, for which doubtless its advocates can find much to say. Whether Jesus himself intended to found, or foresaw the founding, of a new religion apart and distinct from Judaism, is, however, another question. It is, in part, clearly dependent upon the views which Jesus held as to the end of the world. If he thought that that end was near, he can hardly have also intended to found a new religion and a new religious community. Taken all in all, it seems probable that Jesus was *not* the conscious founder of the Christian Church. He was, and meant to remain, a Jew. Or rather the question of separating from the Synagogue never presented itself to his mind. He wanted to purify, to quicken, to amend, but not to break away and make a fresh beginning. He continued the work of Amos, Hosea, and Isaiah. His Kingdom of God, from one point of view, was a reformed Judaism. And possibly it may come to pass that in his teaching there may be found a reconciliation or meeting point between a Reformed or Liberal Judaism and a frankly Unitarian Christianity of the distant future. *That* Judaism and *that* Christianity may find that they differ in name, in accent, and in memories, rather than essentially or dogmatically. *That* Judaism and *that* Christianity may both claim Jesus as their own.[10]

DID JESUS SEEK THE SALVATION OF HIS ENEMIES?

To seek and save the lost was doubtless one of the objects which, as he believed and truly believed, God had commissioned him to discharge. And of how much goodness and self-sacrifice through the ages has not the 'imitation of Christ' in this regard been the source! It has been the motive for innumerable deeds of patient heroism, and has redeemed much sinfulness, and restored many wanderers from virtue and goodness to God. But how strange it is that Jesus himself did not realise that if this was the Son of Man's mission, it should have been applied, and it was applicable, to the Scribe and the Pharisee as well as to the outcast and the tax-collector. Had not the Scribe and Pharisee souls to save? And if they opposed the new teacher, was it not his business, on his own principles, to return the soft answer which removes wrath? But so it was and so it is. To follow the ideal when it is personally distasteful is ever the hardest thing for a mortal man. And so strange is the human heart in its casuistry, that Jesus probably had no idea that he was violating his own principles. Though he taught that it was the 'Pharisees and Scribes' who were really lost, he made no genuine effort to win them over or to save them. By his denunciations – assuming them to be genuine – he only deepened their antagonism, and from his point of view made the lost souls still more certainly lost. If he saved some, he destroyed others, or at least permitted, and foretold, their assured destruction. And the Church has followed in the footsteps of their Master. She too has both reclaimed and rejected, saved and destroyed. She has indeed sought out the lost when they were willing to agree with her dogmas, but directly they did not see eye to eye with her in all things, she has scattered ruin and ban, fulminated and destroyed. She has persecuted the heretic on earth, and proclaimed his eternal damnation in hell.[11]

THE DEATH OF JESUS AND THE SUFFERING OF THE JEWS

Those who believe in a God of righteousness can only bow their heads in awed and yet truthful submission at the strangely mixed means, which He takes for the progress of mankind, at the painful and involved interconnection of good and evil. In spite of the endless misery which was to come upon the Jews because of the death of Jesus; in spite of the false theology and the persecutions and sore evils (apart wholly from the Jewish misery); in spite of the wrongs which were done to liberty, to enlightenment, and to toleration by the Christian Church – one yet sees that the death of Jesus, even as his life, was of immense benefit to the world. Christianity, as we know it, and as Paul made it, was due to his death as much as, if not more than, to his life. Some fundamental truths of Judaism (though not all of them) have been taught to a large part of the world by Christianity; and while in some directions it has obscured those truths, in others it has expanded them. That this might be done, the 'chosen people' has had to suffer. For the law of election seems to go even further than Amos realised, though what he said was sufficiently startling and revolutionary. For Amos said: 'You only have I known of all the inhabitants of the earth; therefore I will visit upon you your iniquities' (Amos 3:2). But even this is not enough. Nineteen centuries of suffering compel us to realise that for some august reason or purpose we must say, 'You have I called: therefore you shall suffer undeservedly.'

The precise proportion of responsibility which belongs to any section of the Jews of Jerusalem for the death of Jesus, must always remain doubtful and uncertain. But the probability, as we have seen, is that the Sadducean priesthood, perhaps backed up by some leading Rabbis, was responsible, together with the Romans, for his death. Yet what matters this, so far as God is concerned? We are disposed to find a difficulty in the 'third or fourth generation' of the second commandment. Yet, if the death of Jesus had been unanimously voted by the entire Jewish people with the votes taken in a plebiscite or referendum, what difference would it make? Third or fourth generation! Why, there have been fifty generations! And the roll is not yet ended, and there seems no prospect of its close. For in substitution of the Master's command, 'You shall love your enemies', there has been forged another: 'Ye shall hate your enemies to the fiftieth or sixtieth generation.'

But this is the will of God in His scheme for the progress of the world. We do not understand why. But the Jews have ever to realize that they have received the consecration of supremest suffering, and that they still in many lands remain the hunted, hated, wounded, but deathless witnesses of God.[12]

THE PERSECUTIONS OF THE EARLY CHRISTIANS

Now the accounts which we have of Jewish persecution of the new religion all of them emanate from a period when the mission to the Jews themselves had failed. It is far-fetched to suppose that the Synagogue became vicious because jealous of the transference of Paul's propaganda to the Gentiles. The Jewish sources have a good deal to say about Christians, but almost invariably it is *Jewish* Christians that are the object of castigation. Even supposing that in the course of time some passages were censored or suppressed, yet it is assuredly an extraordinary fact that it is scarcely possible to cite a single clear attack against Gentile Christianity in the early Rabbinic literature. The Synagogue was concerned with its own internal affairs; it had to keep itself free from *minuth* (a phrase which, though not always identical with, in the passages now under review refers to Judeo-Christianity); and its endeavours were directed primarily to self-defence ... The Synagogue had far less quarrel with Gentile Christianity, and until the organized Church had become imperial and was in a position and displayed the will to persecute the Synagogue, Christianity as such was not the object of much attention, still less of attack ...

The protagonists of a new movement, and their heirs and historians in later ages, are always inclined to mistake opposition for persecution. A Jewish reader of Acts, making allowance for Paul's temperament, refusing to accept as literal his account of the persecutions he inflicted as Saul or suffered as Paul, sees some of the facts in a different perspective. Paul, to take the incidents which lead up to the change in his attitude, visited the Synagogue at Antioch of Pisidia on the Sabbath day. After the lessons had been read, he received a courteous invitation to speak a word of exhortation to the people. He used the opportunity to discourse of the divinity of Jesus (Acts 13:15). The Jews 'contradicted the things which were spoken by Paul' (verse 45). This is the essential fact. In self-defence, the Jews put before their own brethren their objections to Paul's teachings. There is no hint of impeding Paul until he persistently preached Christianity in the Synagogues. Had Paul from the first directed his aims to the conversion of Gentiles the case might have been quite otherwise. One wonders what would be the fate of a zealous Imam who should on a Sunday appear at St Paul's Cathedral and, after the lesson from the Gospel, urge the assembled Anglicans to prefer the claims of Mohammed to those of Jesus, on the ground that the coming of Mohammed had been prophesied by Christ.

It is this inability to place himself at the Jewish point of view that sets even Harnack among those who give a wrong colour to the facts, and persist in alleging that in the first and second centuries there was a steady and insidious campaign by the Synagogue against Gentile Christianity. In his *Expansion of Christianity* (English translation, Vol. I, p. 65) Harnack has a very strong passage on the subject, which is quoted and relied upon again and again as though it were history instead of conjecture. He says: 'The hostility of the Jews appears on every page of Acts, from chapter 13 onwards. They tried to hamper every step of the Apostle's work among the Gentiles; they stirred up the masses and the authorities in every country against him; systematically and officially they scattered broadcast horrible charges against the Christians, which played an important part in the persecutions as early as the reign of Trajan; they started calumnies against Jesus; they provided heathen opponents of Christianity with literary ammunition; unless the evidence is misleading, they instigated the Neronic outburst against the Christians; and as a rule whenever bloody persecutions are afoot in later days, the Jews are either in the background or the foreground.'

To begin with, this generalization altogether overlooks the evidence of Acts 17. At Athens, Paul reasons with the Jews in the Synagogue, but also with any whom he met in the Agora. 'And certain also of the Epicurean and Stoic philosophers encountered him. And some said, "What would this babbler say?" Others said, "He seems to be a preacher of foreign divinities."' Where is the Jewish instigation here? Stoics and Epicureans had their own case. When a Rabbi came into conversation with Greek philosophers, his purpose was to uphold the 'wise men of the Jews' against 'the ancients of Athens'. E. Hatch has some admirable remarks in his Hibbert Lectures on heathen opponents of Christianity. But Harnack does more than accuse the Jews of literary animosity. They were the open or secret prompters of persecutions, particularly those of which Nero was guilty.

For such strong accusations one has the right to demand equally strong evidence. But Harnack fails to provide it. It has been left to P. Corssen in recent times to find in Josephus the instigator of Nero's savagery. Harnack was not able to suggest so simple a solution. '*Unless the evidence is misleading*, they instigated the Neronic outburst against the Christians,' says Harnack. When pressed as to his meaning, he admits that he is relying solely on conjecture.

In a later passage (Vol. II, p. 116) he returns to the same charge, but in the text modifies his assertion to the less emphatic statement that 'the Neronic persecution' was '*probably* instigated by the Jews,' and on the word *probably* he has this footnote: 'Without this hypothesis it is scarcely possible, in my opinion, to understand the persecution.' The Jews are charged in the most violent terms with instigating the Neronic persecution, and the only evidence adduced by the author of the charge is that he needs the hypothesis to explain the event! Others have been quite able to explain the event without this hypothesis, and without the equally unfounded guess that Nero was induced to his cruelty against the Christians by female Jewish influence at court. Neither Tacitus, nor Suetonius, nor any of the original sources for the history of Rome has a hint of Jewish complicity. And if there is nothing but conjecture for the specific cases alleged by Harnack, still less can his general indictment ('as a rule whenever bloody persecutions are afoot in later days, the Jews are either in the background or the foreground') be held justified by anything like historical evidence.

There is only one single period at which it would appear likely that some active persecution occurred. That was the age of Bar Cochba, when national feeling ran high, and the leader of the revolt against Hadrian may as Justin states (*Apology*, Vol. I, 31) have directed his animosity (Justin says nothing of 'bloody' persecution, his language only points to the ordinary judicial flagellation though he has over-coloured the picture) against those Jews who had accepted Christianity and refused to join Aqiba in recognizing Bar Cochba as the Messiah. There is no question here of Gentile Christians; the objects of the rebel leader's wrath were those of his own countrymen who refused to join the rebellion. The animosity is comparable to that felt by many Englishmen against Conscientious Objectors during the recent War. Tarphon and Meir, who were among the Rabbis who helped to repress the Christian movement, were also concerned simply and solely with the heresy within their own body; the danger was that this *minuth* was present secretly in some of the synagogues. It is a very plausible theory that the paragraph introduced at the end of the first century into the Liturgy (in the Eighteen Benedictions) against the *minim* was designed to separate the sheep from the goats and compel the *minim* to declare themselves ...

The same conclusion must be drawn from the citations which are often quoted from the Church Fathers in evidence of the animosity displayed by the Jews against the early Christians. In very few of these citations can be found any such evidence. For the most part they merely show that the Jewish authorities took energetic steps to warn *their fellow-Jews* against the new faith. The language of Justin is too exaggerated to be taken literally. He goes so far as to protest that the Jews aided 'evil demons and the host of the devil' against the lives of the saints *(Dialogue,* 131). Such phraseology is obviously that of an advocate rather than of a historian. In reality, what the Jewish authorities did was, more or less, *defensive.* That this is so may be seen most clearly from the very passage on which Harnack chiefly relies for the opposite view, viz, that the Jews were occupied in an anti-Christian campaign throughout the Gentile world. 'By far the most important notice', says Harnack, 'is that preserved by Eusebius (on Isaiah 18:1 ff.) although its source is unfortunately unknown.' (It may be suggested that the source is Justin, *Dialogue,* 117.) The passage, 'by far the most important' authority for the oft-repeated charge as to the all-pervading efforts of the Jews at home to assail the Christians of the Gentile world, runs as follows: 'We have found in the writings of the ancients that Jerusalem priests and elders of the Jewish people sent letters to all the Jews everywhere traducing the doctrine of Christ, as a new heresy alien to God, and admonishing them in letters not to accept it.' If such encyclicals were actually sent so extensively as this, Eusebius' ancient authority merely states that the central authorities at Jerusalem sent warnings *to their own brethren* in the diaspora exhorting them to turn a deaf ear to the efforts of Christian missionaries, in that the new religion was not compatible with Judaism. So far from this being evidence of Jewish aggression, it is on the contrary a statement of efforts needed for self-defence. The same is the true inference to be drawn from the majority of the complaints of the fathers. The Jewish defence of Judaism sometimes assumed the form of an attack on Christianity, and this attack would not invariably be fair or in good taste. But only in the rarest cases is it directly alleged (e.g. Origen, *Against Celsus*, 6:27) that the Jews initiated specific charges, and it is noteworthy that Origen does not assert this of his own experience. Mostly the complaint is that the Jews actually defended themselves by placing before their brethren the fundamental objections to Christianity from the Jewish side, and these arguments were also, no doubt, sometimes adopted by heathen opponents of Christianity ... In fact Celsus was as bitter an assailant of Judaism as he was of Christianity. Nay the latter was the object of his scorn just *because* it grew out of the former (1:2). As Origen himself says (1:22): Celsus 'thinks that he will be able the more easily to establish the falsity of Christianity, if, by assailing its origin in Judaism, he can show that the latter also is untrue.' Jews could hardly have been behind Celsus! And the same is true of other Gentile assailants.[13]

JESUS, THE RABBIS AND PROPHECY

An essential feature of the prophet is the sense of commission and vocation. He is called by God to deliver a message, and thus stands towards God in a certain special relation. What he speaks he speaks in God's name, and he believes that it is the divine spirit which impels him to his work and directs his words. Jesus does not preface his speeches with 'thus saith the Lord', but in the conviction of inspiration, in the assurance that he too was called and chosen by God to do a certain work, he entirely resembles Amos, Isaiah and Ezekiel ... We do, I think, know enough about the Rabbis of the first century AD to say that, however fine and noble their teaching may have been or was, it cannot properly be called prophetic. They were not called prophets, and they could not have properly been called so. However much they may have recognised that, at bottom, the Pentateuchal laws of morality were greater than its laws about sacrifice or 'clean and unclean', they could not, they did not, deal with the subject in the same way and spirit as Jesus. Hillel was ever the servant of the Law, and never its Judge. In a sense he was more consistent than Jesus; but for that very reason he was less prophetic. Sabbath conflicts, such as happened to Jesus, could not have happened to him. That is why, or that is 'one' why, the production of parallels from the teaching of Hillel with the teaching of Jesus is mostly futile. The spirit is different. The prophetic touch is present in one case and absent in the other, and it is the prophetic touch which makes the difference.

It is true that Jesus was called a prophet mainly because ... he announced with the assurance of conviction, with inspiration and therefore with authority, the imminence of the Judgment and of the Kingdom. In this, too, he resembles the ancient prophets, and he may indeed be said to have combined the parts of Amos and of the Second Isaiah. He announces doom to the unrepentant and the wicked: he comforts the repentant and the seekers; the afflicted and the poor; the humble and the yearning. And in this more primary sense of the word he was, if not so original as in the other, yet also unlike his Rabbinic contemporaries. The combination at least was new: Jesus was teacher, pastor, and prophet in one, and in this combination too lies something of his originality.[14]

JESUS, THE RABBIS AND A FORGIVING GOD

It would be very difficult to answer the question: who teaches, on the whole, a more forgiving conception of God – the Jesus of the Synoptic Gospels or the Rabbis? We have a number of exquisite and tender sayings such as Matt. 18:14,[15] but these are counterbalanced by Matt. 25:41–46[16] and similar passages, where 'aeonian' and painful hell is declared to be the lot of the wicked. We have also such a hard and gloomy utterance as that in Matt. 7:13–14,[17] which seems to teach that those who perish shall be far more numerous than those who shall be saved. We have a cruel denunciation and threat, such as Matt. 11:20–24.[18] But it has also to be recognised that the main strain of the Synoptic teaching is (a) sound as regards the purely ethical tests for salvation or destruction, as the case may be; (b) of a less nationalistic tendency than that of the Rabbis; (c) less burdened by verse in the O.T. of a low ethical quality; and (d) more definitely solicitous for the 'little ones' or the 'simple.' The new particularism of creed had hardly begun to rear its ugly head in the Synoptic Gospels. The Rabbis were more 'nationalist' than Jesus: their hostility to the idolator and the alien (who for them mean so largely and often the oppressors and the 'Romans') was more intense and more constant. As regards sinners in Israel, so long as these were not anti-Rabbinic 'enemies,' the Rabbis were, I should think, no less eager for their repentance than Jesus, though they did not, like him, seek them out and try actively to convert them to righteousness. The O.T. burden was, however, very grave for them. It reinforced the hatreds and animosities of the natural man. Jesus did not, I should imagine, know the O.T. in the same wonderful way that they did. Nor did he regard it in the same way. He had present in his consciousness and memory only those verses which had specially struck him, or which chimed in with his own teaching. He was more independent and inspired. The Rabbis knew the O.T. too painfully well, and to them, unfortunately, all the statements about God in the O.T. were almost equally true. Thus, if God is said to 'hate' Edom, if he is said to 'laugh at' the wicked, all of whom he will at the last 'destroy' (and we know that there are many similar passages), all these sayings must somehow be true – just as true as the loving and beautiful and tender sayings, and they all came in most conveniently, and were most 'handy,' when nationalistic and particularistic animosities craved biblical sanction. On the whole, the Rabbis come out of this great difficulty fairly well; but if both Jesus and they equally believe in hell and in its eternity (and I see no difference here), there is, sometimes, in the Rabbinic conception, more zest attributed to God in the destruction of enemies who are both his enemies and Israel's.[19]

CHRISTIANITY AND JEWISH LEGALISM

Under the influence of Paul, and of Luther and of other teachers of the Reformation period, there is no doctrine against which many Protestant theologians fulminate more violently than the doctrine of reward. They do not mind punishment; they could hardly mind it, when the extended use of the Gehenna and Hell from the Gospel onwards right down to Luther and Calvin and up to modern times, is borne in mind, but they hate what they call eudaemonism – so much good action paid for by so much reward – and they assert that reward is the sheet anchor of Judaism, and especially of the Rabbis. Man earns his reward in Judaism: the grace of God gives undeserved and unearned beatitude in Christianity. The result is, in one sense, the same: both Judaism and Christianity assume that the good and believing will enjoy bliss, but what is earned reward to the one is a free gift to the other. Legalism, the hated red rag and unclean thing to Lutheran theologians, involves reward. Legalism and eudaemonism go together. It was necessary to smash legalism to get rid of the bribery and degradation of reward.

There is an exaggeration in all this tilting against reward. It has been shown by Schechter and Abrahams and others that there is not only less 'eudaemonism' in Rabbinic theology than its antagonists would allow, but also that its eudaemonism is tempered by several other and very different strains. It has also been shown that the assurance and even the delineation of reward do not necessarily mean that good acts were performed for the sake of the reward, or that pure and disinterested piety was not as prized and familiar to the Rabbi as to the Christian. The familiar doctrine of *Lishmah* [for its own sake] which ninety-nine out of a hundred German Protestant theologians ignore, or have never heard of, is the best proof that the motive of reward was regarded as the lower and less desirable motive, 'for its own sake' or 'for love' as the higher and more desirable motive. Again, Jesus, who was happily ignorant of these antagonisms and oppositions, was quite ready, every now and then, to use the doctrine of reward, and to enunciate it, as here,[20] in the very strongest and simplest terms. The Protestant theologians try hard to show that he does not really mean what he says, or that somehow his doctrine of reward is wholly different from the Rabbis' doctrine of reward; he is pure, theirs is impure; his is a mere use of popular language, theirs is seriously meant; his is an exquisite statement of the gracious goodness of God, theirs is calculation and bribery – and so on. But for those who stand above the facts these differences are largely the creation of the theologians.

On the other hand, it *is* true both that there is too much of measure for measure and of merit in the Rabbinic literature, and that there are some noble utterances against measure for measure, and against human goodness or the service of God *meriting* reward in the teaching of Jesus ...

But it may be observed of the eudaemonism of Jesus, and

often too of the eudaemonism of the Rabbis, that they are an eudaemonism of a special kind. They do not say, 'Do this, or be this, *because* you will gain a reward,' or 'Do not do this *because* you will be punished.' But they say, 'A certain line of action, a certain disposition of mind, bring happiness now and hereafter.' The result follows necessarily from the cause. It is the law of God. 'Heaven' and happiness follow as certainly from goodness, as their opposites follow from wickedness. The one is not an arbitrarily added reward; the other is not an arbitrarily added punishment. The result is contained in the premise, as surely as the result of health-giving medicines or death-dealing drugs is already contained within them. The bliss of virtue, both 'now' and 'hereafter,' is a continuous state, and not a something added *ab extra* to form a reward and *mutatis mutandis*, the same way be said of vice. Thus the sting of the supposed ' eudaemonism' is removed ...

It is curious that the same charges of eudaemonism and of impure morality, which are levelled by many German Protestant scholars against Judaism and the religion of the Rabbis, are brought by some modern Jewish teachers against Christianity and the religion of Jesus. The Jewish kettle makes a hot retort against the Christian pot. The 'Vergeltungsglaube' of Judaism and the Rabbis is denounced up hill and down dale by the German Protestant theologians. The charge is that the one single motive or end for well-doing in Judaism is the hope of reward or the fear of punishment. The Jewish critic of Christianity and of the teaching of Jesus says that, though the *scene* of the reward or punishment is shifted to the life beyond the grave – to heaven and hell – the end or purpose of well-doing in Christianity and in the teaching of Jesus is that 'thy Father in heaven may reward thee in heaven. Moreover, the teaching is selfish and anti-social; the one end sought is personal salvation. Nothing matters so long as you save your own soul: that is, and should be, the one overmastering care or object: that you, the individual, should avoid the pains of hell and secure the beatitudes of heaven.

How curious that each set of critics make practically the same accusation. The historian, who is free from prejudice, will agree that there is *some* force in both accusations: of the Christian against Judaism and of the Jew against Christianity. *Some* force but not more.[21]

THE TELLING SILENCE OF CHRISTIAN SCHOLARSHIP

With very few honourable exceptions the Christian scholar, and more especially the German Protestant scholar, simply ignores what Jewish scholars have to say. If he would argue the point, if he would discuss, if he would deign to notice us, there would be some pleasure and interest. But what on earth is the good of returning to the charge when no enemy appears? Is it possible that what the Jewish scholars say is so silly, so contemptibly prejudiced, so utterly erroneous, that it is really too much to expect that any Christian scholar can notice it? But, after all, are we necessarily so much more prejudiced on our side than the Christian scholars are on theirs? If we write on the New Testament or speak about Jesus and Paul, do we ignore the great Christian divines? ...

The policy of silence would be less conspicuous and less significant if, Christian scholars never noticed what Jewish scholars had to say about anything whatever. But this is far from being the case. On any other subject than Rabbinic religion and theology, the Jewish scholars are at once sure of a respectful and intelligent attention ... But theology is taboo. Nothing escapes the marvellous ingenuity of a German scholar like Schürer. If a Jewish writer makes some foolish suggestion as to the size and population of a Palestinian city in the Maccabean era Schurer will at all events do that writer the honour of alluding in a footnote to his suggestion as 'völlig unannehmbar' or 'haltungslos'. But let the greatest Rabbinical scholar of the age write a series of epoch-making studies on Rabbinic theology Schurer will not even deign to mention or contradict him.

Far less important matters than Rabbinic theology are worried about persistently. However there are special reasons why this particular matter must not be allowed to rest; why Jewish writers must continue to plea for discussion and fair consideration of what they have to say. After all, Rabbinic theology has some relation to the early history of Christianity, and it does make some difference whether the Rabbinic religion was good or bad. Is that the real reason why the Christian scholars refuse to listen when so unique a scholar as Schechter addresses? ...

It is easy to see that great confusion would be caused in current opinions if the commonplaces of the theologians were wrong. For suppose, after all, that the Law was not a burden, that the Sabbath was a day of delight, that ceremonies and spirituality, letter and spirit, could, did and do go together, how very awkward the result might be. Then, though Christianity might be a far greater religion than Judaism, there would be two good religions instead of one, two ways of approaching and finding God instead of one. Then though Paul's doctrine might be great and noble, it would not be the only way to salvation then one could be spiritual and commune with God through the Law as well as through the Gospel, then true prayer, self sacrifice and disinterested religion might be the possession of Judaism and Christianity, of living orthodox Jews as well as living orthodox Christians. And surely this would never do. Schechter's articles are highly dangerous: leave them alone! …

Schechter has shown that the God of the Rabbis was not 'remote', that their righteousness was not 'hollow' that they knew the highest meaning of prayer, of holiness, of disinterested love of God. These things he, the foremost scholar of his age, has to my thinking shown. But even if he has not shown them, he has produced material so new and large, so interesting, so counter to current conceptions and popular verdicts, that it surely demands consideration. Let it be refuted, if possible, by all means, but let it not be ignored.[22]

PARTICULARISM AND UNIVERSALISM:
PAUL AND THE RABBIS

The great and momentous contribution of Paul to religious development was his pronounced and emphatic universalism. He broke down the barrier (it is true by erecting another) between Jew and Gentile and he put all believers in Christ upon an equality, whether they were Gentiles or whether they were Jews. That in *his* sense we do not believe in Christ, that to us all men are alike God's children, whatever their creed, must not blind us to the greatness of his achievement. We must not be capricious or hesitating in acknowledgment and praise. 'Is God the God of Jews only? Is He not the God of Gentiles also?' 'For there is no distinction between Jew and Greek for the same

Lord is Lord of all and is rich unto all that call upon Him'
(Romans 3:29, 10:12). Before and 'in' Christ, or, as we should
say, before and with God, there cannot be, and there is not,
'Greek and Jew, circumcision and uncircumcision, barbarian,
Scythian, bondman, freeman, male and female' (Col. 3:11 cf. Gal.
3:28).

To this universalism, in spite of its partial limitation to those
who believe in the Messiahship of Jesus, the Liberal Jew cannot
refuse to render his homage. He will not refuse to recognize its
enormous significance, or to realize that, whether we like the
fact or no, it established a world religion. Judaism had, so far,
not been able to solve the puzzle of the universal God and the
national cult. Paul cut the knot. He cut it, it is true, by setting
up dogmas which darkened the purity of monotheism, and
opened the door for many subsequent evils both in religion and
morality; but yet he cut it. We will not deny to him his mead
of glory.

Yet it is only fair to point out that neither Rabbinic particularism nor Pauline universalism was complete. In Rabbinism there
are universalist elements of great moment and significance; in
Paulinism, of no less moment and significance, there are elements of particularism. Liberal Judaism has combined the good
elements, and has rejected the evil elements, of both Rabbinism
and Paulinism.

Paul doubtless declared that in the Messiah Jesus there was
neither Jew nor Greek: he made the new religion independent
of race. He broke down the shackles which had so greatly
hindered the diffusion of Judaism beyond the limits of a single
nation. He showed that religion was something gloriously
wider than any single people. But, in destroying one kind of
shackles, he created another. In shattering old fetters, he forged
new ones. And these new fetters, though related to morality,
were yet distinct from it. All who believe in the Messiah Jesus
are on an equality, be their race, their social condition, or their
sex, what it may. But what of those who do not believe in him?
These are left in, or relegated to, the outer darkness. And just
as the Jews were tempted to declare (in order to save the moral
situation) that every heathen was of necessity a sinner, so were
Christians soon tempted to describe those who rejected – and
even those who were ignorant of – Christ. The unbeliever not

because he is of one particular race, but in virtue of his unbelief, is a child of perdition and sin. And, in some ways, this particularism, when 'faith' is partly degraded to an intellectual assent to certain theological dogmas and subtleties, is more shocking, more calumniating to the goodness of God, than the particularism of the Rabbis.

Some dubious exceptions were made for Socrates and Plato, and a few others of the heroes of Greece and of Rome, but neither the ancient nor the Medieval Church ever enunciated the doctrine 'the righteous, be their religious beliefs what they may, have a share in the blessedness of the world to come'.

The Rabbis, however, to their great credit and glory, broke down their nationalist particularism, even while the credal particularism of the Church was hardly penetrated by any serious breach. In an early Rabbinic treatise we find the immortal saying: 'The righteous of all nations shall have a share in the world to come.' In their words: not genealogy, but conduct, is the passport to heaven. It is true that a Rabbi could have hardly have conceived a man as righteous who did not believe in One God. But, nevertheless, not religious belief, but conduct is made the condition. The righteous: he it is who is 'saved'. Righteousness – not race, not belief – that is what God cares for, looks to and demands.

And this saying, so great and august in its simplicity, won its way gradually more and more, and became the official doctrine of the Synagogue from comparatively early times. Long before any Church said: 'It matters not what a man believes God looks to his deeds', Judaism, without making the antithesis in so many words, had asserted the doctrine which it implies. Rightly may Rabbinic apologists quote over and over again this single illuminating sentence. It did not at first mean all that they make it mean: to attempt to find modern toleration in the Talmud is absurd and unhistoric, but nevertheless this single sentence meant a noble meaning even to its first author, and it gradually grew to mean more and more.

The universalism of Liberal Judaism derives, therefore, both from Paul and from the Rabbis, though it has moved far beyond both. For to us universalism does not stop short before the redemption of every human soul: and if we clothe our faith in sensuous terms, we should say, 'The sinners of every faith and nation shall have a share in the world to come.'[23]

A COMMENT ON MATTHEW 25:41

Then shall he also say unto them on the left hand, Depart
from me, ye accursed, into the everlasting fire.

Such passages as Matt. 25:41 should make theologians exces-
sively careful of drawing beloved contrasts between the Old
Testament and the New. We find even liberal theologian Dr
Fosdick saying: 'From Sinai to Calvary – was ever a record of
progressive revelation more plain or more convincing? The
development begins with Jehovah disclosed in a thunderstorm
on a desert mountain, and it ends with Christ saying: "God is
Spirit: and they that worship Him must worship Him in spirit
and truth"; it begins with a war-god leading his partisans to
victory, and it ends with men saying, "God is love; and he that
abideth in love abideth in God, and God abideth in him"; it
begins with a provincial deity loving his tribe and hating its
enemies, and it ends with the God of the whole earth worshipped "by a great multitude, which no man could number, out of
every nation, and of all the tribes and peoples and tongues"; it
begins with a God who commands the slaying of the Amale-
kites, "both man and woman, infant and suckling", and it ends
with a Father whose will it is that not "one of these little ones
should perish"; it begins with God's people standing afar off
from his lightenings and praying that he might not speak to
them lest they die and it ends with men going into their inner
chambers, and, having shut the door, praying to their father
who is in secret" (*Christianity and Progress*, 1922, p. 209.) Very
good. No doubt such a series can be arranged. Let me now
arrange a similar series. From the Old Testament to the New
Testament – was there ever a record of retrogression more plain
or more convincing? It begins with, "Have I any pleasure at all
in the death of him that dieth?"; it ends with "Begone from me,
ye doers of wickedness." It begins with, "The Lord is slow to
anger and plenteous in mercy"; it ends with, "Fear Him who
is able to destroy both body and soul in Gehenna." It begins
with, "I will dwell with him that is of a contrite spirit to revive
him"; it ends with, "Narrow is the way which leads to life, and
few there be who find it." It begins with, "I will not contend
for ever; I will not always be wrath;" it ends with, "Depart, ye
cursed, into the everlasting fire." It begins with, "Should I not

have pity on Nineveh, that great city?"; it ends with, "It will be more endurable for Sodom on the day of Judgement than for that town." It begins with, "The Lord is good to all who call upon Him"; it ends with, "Whoever speaks against the Holy Spirit, there is no forgiveness whether in this world or the next." It begins with, "The Lord will wipe away tears from off all faces; he will destroy death forever"; it ends with, "They will throw them into the furnace of fire; there is the weeping and the gnashing of teeth."' And the one series would be as misleading as the other.[24]

NOTES

1. Claude Montefiore, *The Bible for Home Reading*, Vol. 2, London: Macmillan (1896), pp. 778–81.
2. Claude Montefiore, *Liberal Judaism and Hellenism*, London: Macmillan (1918), pp. 124–8.
3. Claude Montefiore, *The Synoptic Gospels*, London: Macmillan (1910), Vol. 1, pp. cxxxvi–cxxxviii.
4. 'And he called the people to him again, and said to them, "Hear me, all of you, and understand: there is nothing outside a man which by going into him can defile him; but the things which come out of a man are what defile him."'
5. 'I tell you the truth, whatever you did for the least of these brothers of mine, you did for me.'
6. V. 33: 'He will put the sheep on his right and the goats on his left'; v. 41: 'Then he will say to those on his left, "Depart from me, you who are cursed, into the eternal fire prepared for the devil and his angels"'; v. 46: 'Then they will go way to eternal punishment, but the righteous to eternal life.'
7. Montefiore, *The Synoptic Gospels*, Vol. 1, pp. xxiv–xxvi.
8. 'Do not seek revenge or bear a grudge against one of your people, but love your neighbour as yourself. I am the Lord.'
9. Israel Abrahams, *Studies in Pharisaism and the Gospels*, Cambridge: Cambridge University Press (1917), pp. 33–9.
10. Montefiore, *The Synoptic Gospels*, Vol. 1, p. cxxxv.
11. Ibid., Vol. 2, p. 456.
12. Ibid., Vol. 1, pp. 395–6.
13. Israel Abrahams, *Studies in Pharisaism*, pp. 56–62.
14. Montefiore, *The Synoptic Gospels*, Vol. 1, pp. cxx–cxxi.
15. 'So it is not in the will of my Father who is in heaven that one of these little ones should perish.'
16. 'Then he will say to those at his left hand, "Depart from me, you cursed, into the eternal fire prepared for the devil and his angels; for I was hungry and you gave me no food, I was thirsty and you gave me no drink; I was a stranger and you did not welcome me, naked and you did not clothe me, sick and in prison and you did not visit me." Then they will also answer, "Lord, when did we see thee hungry or thirsty or a

stranger or naked or sick in prison, and did not minister to thee?" Then
he will answer them, "Truly, I say to you, as you did it not to one of the
least of these, you did it not to me." And they will go way into eternal
punishment, but the righteous into eternal life.'

17. 'Enter by the narrow gate; for the gate is wide and the way is easy, that
    leads to life and those who find it are few.'
18. 'Then he began to upbraid the cities where most of his mighty works had
    been done, because they did not repent. Woe to you Chorazin! Woe to
    you, Bethsaida! For if the mighty works had been done in Tyre or Sidon,
    they would have repented long ago in sackcloth and ashes. But I tell you,
    it shall be more tolerable on the day of judgement for Tyre and Sidon
    than for you. And you Capernaum, will you be exalted to heaven? You
    shall be brought down to Hades. For if the mighty works done in you
    had been done in Sodom, it would have remained until this day. But I
    tell you that it shall be more tolerable on the day of judgement for the
    land of Sodom than for you.'

19. Claude Montefiore, *Rabbinic Literature and Gospel Teachings*, London:
    Macmillan (1930), pp. 261–2.
20. Montefiore is commenting on Matthew 5:1–2.
21. Montefiore, *The Synoptic Gospels*, Vol. 2, pp. 40–2.
22. Montefiore, The *Hibbert Lectures on the Origin of Religion as Illustrated by
    the Ancient Hebrews*, London: Williams and Norgate, Vol. 1, pp. 335–6.
23. Montefiore, *Liberal Judaism and Hellenism*, pp. 119–22.
24. Montefiore, *Synoptic Gospels*, Vol. 2, pp. 326–7.

4

Rabbinic Judaism

A host of examples could be brought from the Talmud to illustrate the high ethical demands which the Rabbis laid on those who would fulfil the requirements of the good life in the religious sense. They would include the injunctions about charity. Most significant perhaps are the Rabbinic prescriptions for those in commerce and industry who would live religiously. They have to do in their dealings with others more than the law requires, or practical reason could justify. God, it is said, examines the pious strictly; presumably more strictly than others. They not only have to fulfil ethical obligations most scrupulously, but it is required of them to be more than just to others and to accept less than justice for themselves.

Two important corollaries follow from the identification of the ethically good life with the religious life. First, the religious life, according to Judaism, is not a special kind of life but the ordinary life lived religiously. That explains the absence of Jewish monastic orders. The nearest approach to monasticism among Jews was in the lives devoted to the study of the Law. The study of the Law was incumbent on all Jews; and there was a time when all Jews added it to their vocations in ways best suited to their respective intellectual abilities. Conversely, students of the Law were expected and urged to have some trade. Rabbis attached a high value to manual work, both for its personal and social value. 'Great is handicraft for it honours those who do it. He who enjoys the fruit of his labours is greater than the fearer of heaven.' One Rabbi especially commended farming. In the Testaments of the Twelve Patriarchs, Issachar urges his sons to engage in it. In the saying I have quoted, the Rabbis of Jamnia put the work of the peasant on a level with that of the scholar. No occupation is too humble for earning a livelihood. Some Rabbis were themselves engaged in humble occupations. Torah (study of the Law), or learning, must go with a worldly occupation. Though some Rabbis dissented, it was the general Rabbinic view that students of the Law were not exempt from ordinary pursuits by which men earn their living, and from other activities by which they could share in the life of the community.

Rabbinic, Pharisaic, literature contains many and severe condemnations of those who devote themselves to study without deeds, contemplation without action; and also severe condemnation of those who use their knowledge of the Law as a means of livelihood, instead of a trade. Obviously the ideal combination of an ordinary occupation and the study of the Law could not always be carried out in practice. There were always some, like the great masters of the Law, who devoted all their time to study and teaching, much in the way of modern university professors. As time went on, and life became more complicated, and occupations demanded longer and greater exertions, Jewish communities had to rely for religious guidance more and more on official Rabbis, experts in the Law, who had to devote all their time to it, in order that they might instruct the people in its requirements, or judge their disputes in accordance with its laws. And young men who wanted to become learned in the Law would devote themselves wholly to its study under the instruction of Rabbis famed for their knowledge. But these Rabbis and students lived ordinary lives. The study of the Law called for special sacrifices, but not for isolation from the world. On the contrary, it must give precedence to good deeds ...

The second corollary from the identification of the good life with the religious life is that all which rightly belongs to the normal life is entitled to a place in the good life. It can be raised to the highest service of God. The special acts of worship, which Judaism requires, can be performed in the normal course of life, imparting to the whole of it an atmosphere of holiness. Therefore Judaism does not make asceticism, the rejection of all physical pleasures, a condition of the religious life.

The religious life is, therefore, the ordinary life, engaged in normal pursuits, transfigured, exalted, directed, and infused throughout, by obedience to the law of God out of love for him. Whatever a man's occupation, so long as it is ethically fit, it can be exalted into the highest form of religious life. Consecration

of the whole of a man's waking existence to the service of God
... was for the Pharisee the way of the perfect life. It is the way
to fulfil the commandment, 'Ye shall be perfect with the Lord
your God' (Deuteronomy 18:13); and it remains the Jewish ideal
of the good life. By this ideal the higher morality is precipitated
into the ordinary life. The man who lives the good life is called
either *chasid*, the pious one, or *tsaddik*, the righteous one. Both
have been applied, in the Talmud and in later Judaism, to those
who, by loving and loyal devotion to God in thought and
conduct, established themselves, according to the judgement of
others, completely in the right relation with him. And those to
whom these high titles were given lived in the world, fulfilling,
again in the judgement of others, to the utmost the Jewish ideal
of the good life.

To sum up, Judaism does not offer two forms of the good
life, one for ordinary men and women engaged in ordinary
pursuits, and one for those who want to devote themselves to
a completely religious life, differentiated from ordinary life not
only by the degree of its religious quality, but also by its negative relation to this world and this life. For Judaism there is only
one kind of good life, the life guided and dominated throughout by religion; and the best life is the life that realizes most
nearly the religious ideal of faith and righteousness. Judaism
does not, therefore, take human life out of the world to make
it religious, but it brings religion into human life in the world
to exalt it, to sanctify it. It requires ethically a positive attitude
to this life and this world, with a positive effort to realize
goodness here and now. This does not in any way obscure the
possible reality of another life and another world, but only
affirms the reality and worth of this life and this world. Because
God's will can be done on earth, the life on earth can express
and realize an eternal quality and value.[1]

HOW FAR HAVE THE RABBIS ADVANCED BEYOND THE
OLD TESTAMENT?

Such a question, so reasonable to us, would to them have
seemed a blasphemy. As to them, roughly speaking, everything
in the Sacred Scriptures was on one level of supreme excellence,

so all their religion was for them contained in those Scriptures, and they never expressed any view, or enunciated any doctrine, which they did not seek to justify or substantiate by some biblical passage or utterance. They merely drew out what was already there. To us it would be very doleful to think that there was no religious progress in Judaism for, say, 500 years, and, as a matter of fact, there was a good deal. Not only were several quite new conceptions put forward – an advance direct and clear-cut – but some implicit things in the Scriptures were made explicit, some occasional teachings of value became more frequent, and some indefinite or casually advanced ideas, became definite and dogmatic.

I have already indicated that the drawing out of every biblical idea ran a danger of cutting both ways. For one can obviously draw out the 'low' as well as the 'high', the bad as well as the good. The Rabbis did not entirely escape this danger. Some, at any rate, of the imperfections and crudities of the Hebrew Scriptures were elaborated and hardened by the Rabbis, as for example the divine partiality for Israel, and the doctrine of tit for tat. This is unfortunate. For when the Old Testament is what we now call 'particularist', it is so usually in a simple, primitive, unreflecting, and 'natural' way, and this is less upsetting to us than when the Rabbis utter their particularism with reflection, when they make a theory of it or for it, justifying the, to us, unjustifiable. Again, although the Old Testament is for them the word of God, and all is Torah, yet the Pentateuch is pre-eminently the word of God and pre-eminently Torah. The legalism and ceremonialism of the Rabbis are in some respects far better than the legalism and ceremonialism of the Pentateuch; they are less priestly, less primitive, freer from superstitions; but they are also more pronounced, theoretic, elaborate, and pervasive. Things are said, for example, about circumcision which are positively painful to the modern mind, so that we feel inclined to say: better than this advance is the primitiveness of the Pentateuch. Reflected or justified imperfections are worse than naive and spontaneous ones. What is said about hell in the Gospels is bad enough; what is said about hell by St Augustine is much worse. The anthropomorphisms of the Hebrew Bible are often crude and glaring; but they are usually naive and sometimes grand. Some of the anthropomorphisms of the Rabbis jar upon us more. The things which God is made to say and do and think and feel are sometimes so completely on the human level that we are repelled and troubled. Sometimes, too, in doctrine we prefer the primitive spontaneity of the Hebrew Bible. Thus we prefer the simple unreflective tit for tat teachings of the Old Testament to the elaborations of the Rabbis, to the silly idea of such and such divine punishments for such and such sins, of which a shocking and odious instance has found its way from the Mishnah into the orthodox Prayer Book, from which no orthodox authorities have had the manliness or the decency to remove it (cf. Prayer Book p. 121). 'For three transgressions women die in childbirth: because they have been negligent in regard to their periods of separation, in respect to the consecration of the first cake of the dough, and in the lighting of the Sabbath lamp.'

In some ways, therefore, the Hebrew Bible is nearer to us than are the Rabbis. It is also nearer because it is more familiar. Moreover, it contains writers and passages much greater than any writers or passages in the Rabbinical literature. There is nothing from the Rabbis to compare with the Prophets or with Job or with the nobler Psalms. What is splendidly original and full of genius appeals to us more closely. Because the Old Testament is more creative and original than are the Rabbis, we are more drawn to it.

Yet in some respects we are nearer to the Rabbis than the writers of the Bible. And so far as advance and retrogression are concerned, when all is said, the good outweighs the evil. The advance is more conspicuous than the retrogression: the elaboration, the development, the refinement, of the good are larger than those of the 'evil'. Moreover – and this is very pleasing – there are not many instances to be found of the elaborations of the 'evil', where we do not also find some flashes of a vivid sense of the inadequacy or questionableness of the 'evil', and some suddenly interjected sayings in the direction of the good. A 'low' doctrine is flatly contradicted by a 'high' utterance, even though the 'low' teaching is not formally renounced or rejected by the man from whom the 'high' utterance proceeds. Such a formal rejection would be impossible for those who, like the Rabbis, fervently believed in the perfection and inerrancy of the Sacred Scriptures. It is only the modernist who is free.[2]

THE BURDEN OF THE OLD TESTAMENT

The real trouble with the Rabbis, the real check upon religious advance, was the burden of the Old Testament, the burden of the Book. For in spite of some efforts ... to explain away, to reconcile the lower with the higher at the expense at the lower, it remains broadly true that to the Rabbis, the whole Old Testament, and especially the Pentateuch, was true and good and divine: the crudest statements about God were somehow not less true than the noblest; the taboo survivals – the red cow, the waters of impurity, the dietary regulations – were hardly less good, and were certainly no less divine, than 'Thou shalt bear no grudge, and shalt love thy neighbour as thyself' ... Moreover, the burden of the Book acted in another evil direction as well. It stimulated the passions and hatreds and prejudices of the natural man. There was only too much reason why the Rabbis should be intolerant, particularist, and narrow where the gentile and the nations were concerned. Now the Old Testament, instead of checking these tendencies, did, upon the whole, stimulate and intensify them. It gave them the sanctity of religion. It threw over them the veneer of holiness. It gave them divine authority. Thus God is not made usually less partial in Rabbinic literature than He is in the Old Testament. He is usually more partial. He hates the enemies of Israel with an even deeper hatred. And, sometimes, painfully ingenious reasons are given for this partiality which makes it all the worse. The crude anthropomorphisms of the Old Testament are often imitated by the Rabbis. It is true that they do not seem to believe in these anthropomorphisms; but they were dangerous to use, and in Rabbinical literature they are often used in an unseemly and childish manner, which could not have effects for the good. It is even difficult to say how far all the Rabbis were perfectly aware that the anthropomorphisms were anthropomorphisms. They became entangled by them, and the burden of the Book often impaired the purity of their conceptions both of the divine nature and of the divine character. You cannot use crude and childish metaphors too long and too frequently without danger.[3]

RABBINIC PRAYER

It is, one must admit, not easy to speak of a Rabbinic conception of prayer at all. This is true equally of the New Testament, wherein (as with Pharisaism) prayer covers the whole range of thought from the complete acceptance of the Divine Will (Luke 22:42) to the belief in the objective validity of special supplications (James 5:15), from the most rigid brevity (as in the Lord's Prayer) to the acclamation of prayers continual and incessant (Acts 6:4, Eph. 6:18, Thess. 5:17). Theology, in fact, is never systematic while religion is in the formative stages. Pharisaism from the beginning of the first to the end of the fifteenth century remained *in* this formative condition. Rabbinic theology is a syncretism, not a system. To the earliest Pharisees the Bible as a whole, to the later Rabbis the Bible and the traditional literature as a whole, were the sources of inspiration. Hence they adopted and adapted ideas of many ages and many types of mind, and in consequence one may find in Rabbinic Judaism traces of primitive thought side by side with the most developed thought. Especially is this true of prayer. A conspectus of Rabbinic passages on prayer would cover the whole range of evolution, from the spells of a rain-producing magician to the soul-communion of an inspired mystic. A slip in uttering the formulae of prayer was an evil sign on the other extreme, the finest prayer may be made without any formula or word at all.

The Rabbis, again, believed on the one hand in the efficacy of the prolonged prayers of the righteous in general, and on the other hand they, like a certain school of modern Evangelicals, sometimes confided in the possession by gifted individuals of a special faculty for influencing the powers above. Such individuals were mighty men of prayer, able to force their will on a reluctant providence; they would argue, importune, persuade. It has always remained an element in the Jewish theory of prayer that man can affect God; what man does, what be thinks, what he prays, influence the divine action. It is not merely that God cares for man, is concerned with and for man. God's purpose is affected, his intention changed by prayer ... It was generally believed that specific prayer for a specific end might hit the mark.

It *might* hit the mark, but it was not certain to do so. Therein lies the whole saving difference. If Rabbinism is firm in its assertion that prayer *may* be answered, it is firmer still in its denial that prayer *must* be answered. The presumptuous anticipations of Onias the circle-drawer were rebuked by some Rabbis. Haughty prayer, under all circumstances, was obnoxious to the humble spirit of a Hillel. Seeing some of his brethren puffed up by their prayer, as though they were doing God a favour by their praise of him, Hillel reminded them of the uncountable myriads of angelic hosts (Job 25:3) who minister to God, and in comparison with whose majestic adorations man's worship is a puny affair. But when Hillel perceived that his brethren's heart was broken, he changed his note of rebuke against arrogant Israel, to one of encouragement for contrite Israel. Yea, he said, there are these myriads of myriads of angels, but God prefers Israel's praises to theirs; for it is written of David (2 Sam. 23:1) that he was 'the man raised on high, the anointed of the God of Jacob, and the sweet Psalmist of Israel,' and further (Psalm 22:4): 'But Thou art holy, O Thou that art enthroned upon the praises of Israel.' Prayer was efficacious, but its whole efficacy was lost if reliance was placed upon its efficacy. As the Prayer Book version of Psalm 27:16 runs: 'O tarry thou the Lord's leisure: be strong, and He shall comfort thine heart; and put thou thy trust in the Lord.' ...

Against *conditional* prayers, there was strong objection raised. The Rabbis in the Mishnah (Erubin 3:9) refused, for instance to accept the view of Dosa b. Harkinas, that the leader in prayer might say on the New Moon of Tishri, 'Give us strength, O Lord our God, on this New Moon to-day or to-morrow,' in reference to the doubt as to the exact date of the festival. Even more to the point is the Rabbinic denunciation of what they term *Iyyun Tephillah*. The word *Iyyun* means thought, calculation. Sometimes it is used with regard to prayer in a good sense, to connote careful devotion as opposed to mechanical utterance of prescribed formulae. But there is another word for that, viz. *kavvanah*, which may be rendered devotion, than which no more necessary quality can be conceived of in the Rabbinic theory of prayer. But *Iyyun Tephillah* is very often used in a bad sense. Calculation in prayer is the expectation of an answer to prayer as a due claim, and the Rabbis protest with much vehemence against such *expectation* of a divine response to prayer of any kind whatsoever. 'He who prays long and relies on an answer ends in disappointment.' Again: 'To three sins man is daily liable – thoughts of evil, reliance on prayer, and slander.' Thus the expectation of an answer to prayer is an insidious intruder, difficult to avoid, and branded as sin. Perhaps the point can be best illustrated from another side. Not only do the righteous expect no answer to prayer, but they are reluctant to supplicate God for personal benefits. 'The Holy One', we are told, 'yearns for the prayers of the righteous.' God's throne was not established until his children sang songs to him; for there can be no king without subjects. And as God wishes for man's praise, so he longs for man's petitions. But the righteous cannot easily be brought to make petitions. This is the Talmudic explanation of the barrenness of the Patriarchs' wives; God withheld children to compel the reluctant saints to proffer petitions for them. And so also, from a somewhat different point of view, with the whole people of Israel. Why did God bring Israel into the extremity of danger at the Red Sea before effecting a deliverance? Because God longed to hear Israel's prayer, and rather than have Israel silent he made Israel suffer.

There is a hint here of another note; but we can hear it elsewhere more unmistakably. 'Honour the physician before thou hast need of him,' says Ecclesiasticus. This passage is used in the Talmud to criticize the common practice of praying only under the pressure of necessity. 'The Holy One said: Just as it is my office to cause the rain and the dew to fall, and make the plants to grow to sustain man, so art thou bounden to pray before me, and to praise me in accordance with my works; thou shalt not say, I am in prosperity, wherefore shall I pray; but when misfortune befalls me then will I come and supplicate. Before misfortune comes, anticipate and pray.' It will be seen that such passages as this carry us far beyond the conception of prayer as petition. It is an attitude of mind, a constant element of the religious life, independent of the exigencies of specific needs or desires. And that, one may say, on a review of the whole evidence, is a predominant thought in the Rabbinic theory of prayer.[4]

THE LAW AS A SOURCE OF JOY

The Rabbinic literature shows us the Law as an ideal – as the source of joy and happiness and freedom; as the fountain of humility and justice and loving kindness, as the means for obtaining the victory over sin, and for obtaining reconciliation with, and forgiveness from, God.

How, it may be fitly asked, did these good results come about? The answer, I think, may be found in two strangely held beliefs. First, that the Law was the gracious gift of the perfect God, the God who was supreme in loving kindness and in justice and in wisdom. As His gift it shared His perfection ... The second belief was that this wonderful creation of God had been delivered and entrusted to Israel, and that it was Israel's privilege and prerogative, its delight and its happiness, its glory and its honour, as well as its duty and obligation, to observe its commands. This second belief sank deeper and deeper into the hearts of the whole community. It caused a certain amount of objectionable particularism, of pride relative to the gentile, but as it gradually became the belief of the whole community, it did away with the pride of one section of the community over against any other section. For all Israelites tended to become lovers of the Law, all tended to become its humble followers within the limits of their power and to the limits of their frailties. And it was especially the ceremonial portions of the Law which seemed, and were believed, to be the glory and distinction of Israel. The commands against murder, robbery, incest, had been, so it was held, given to all the descendents of Noah, but the ceremonial laws, from the Sabbath down, shall we say, to the fringes on the borders of the garments had been given only to Israel. Why had they been given? All sorts of replies were offered, and the main replies sank deep into the Jewish consciousness. It was held that the ceremonies were to be a test of ready obedience to the inscrutable and not-to-be-criticised will of the Father in heaven. Or, again, that they were intended to connect every part of life – even the most seemingly secular and ordinary parts – with the thought of God. Or that they were meant to beautify life, to add to it adornment and joy, or again to sanctify it, so that through them many passions and instincts might be restrained and hallowed. Or, again, they were meant to discipline and purify men; they were to be – as I must mention again – the counter attraction and retort to the solicitations and temptations of the *Yetzer ha-Ra*, the evil impulse, the source and instigator of iniquity and sin. Nevertheless, it is only fair to say that the distinction between the ceremonial and moral was not lost sight of, and the higher importance, though not the superior beauty, of the moral laws was, upon the whole, effectively maintained. And this happened for several reasons. First, the enactments of the ceremonial law became more and more obeyed by all sections of the community: the class of persons who deliberately disobeyed them, or found them too difficult to observe, became fewer and fewer. Secondly, the Prophets taught Torah as well as the Law, and the teaching of the Prophets was by no means ignored, even though it never entered the heads of the uncritical Rabbis that there was any opposition between the Prophets and the Law. Thirdly, most of the Rabbis were gifted with a strong dose of common sense. However delightful it was to kindle the Sabbath lights, or to observe the dietary laws, the Rabbis knew well enough that justice and mercy were more fundamental commands, more imperative for the well-being of society. Fourthly, another Rabbinic ideal – the imitation of God – tended in the same direction. 'As God is merciful, so you be merciful,' they said: but never, 'As God observes the dietary laws, so do you'; not even, I think, 'As God observes the Sabbath, – for He does observe the Sabbath – so do you'. And the imitation ideal was tremendously strong.[5]

AVOIDING LEGALISM

How was Judaism, which undoubtedly went through a long and intense legal stage, from which it is only now emerging (while even we do not wholly evict law from religion), enabled to avoid, or, at any rate, if it did not wholly avoid, yet largely to triumph over ... dangers [of legalism]. Perhaps partly because of the very nature of the Law itself, and partly because the Sacred Scripture, while it contained the Law (which was regarded as the best and most inspired portion of the whole), yet also contained the Prophets and the Psalms. Or, in other words, because the prophetic teaching was never wholly forgotten, or because the Prophets (inconsistent with the Law as their teaching partly was) had yet partly begotten and produced the Law. No priest, no law; but also, in this case, no prophet, no law.

Now the Law not only included a number of ceremonial enactments, both positive and negative, but as a code it did contain those moral and spiritual dangers which have already been pointed out. On the other hand, the Law included enactments which could only with difficulty be fulfilled in an outward, perfunctory, self-regarding, cheese-paring and selfish way. It asked for the love of neighbour and of the resident alien, it asked for the love of God. And these two laws were moved from early days (let it be noted, not merely by Jesus) to a position of superiority and of primacy. Again, the heart was not wholly quenched even in the Law! The neighbour was not to be hated in the heart; God was to be loved with all the heart. 'Thou shalt not covet': the tenth word could hardly be obeyed except from the heart.

But these are, perhaps, casuistical elegances. The real and fundamental reason I conceive why the dangers were so often and so largely avoided was because the Prophets and the Law together succeeded somehow in making the service of God into a passion. God and His Law were loved, and they were loved not merely because men were asked to love them. God and His Law were so loved that the fulfilment of the Law was carried out for its own sake, and not merely for the sake of reward. And pity and kindness are such characteristics of the Law that they, too, sank deep into the Jewish heart, and were performed for more than reward, and more than outwardly, and more than perfunctorily. God was so loved that the imitation of Him was sought for its own sake. And to imitate God meant pity, meant *chesed*, meant a good and holy life, meant a tender and loving heart. Believe that God is good and love Him, and all the rest follows. Believe that He is pitiful and loving as well as just and holy, and whatever your system, be it legal or be it Pauline, so long as you love Him enough, true goodness and uncalculating unselfishness will ensue.[6]

THE BOOK OF LIFE

Remember us unto life, O King, who delightest in life, and inscribe us in the Book of Life, for Thine own sake, O living God.

This prayer, inserted in the daily service from the New Year till the great fast – from the first to the tenth of Tishri – is of uncertain age. Unmentioned in the Talmud, it meets us for the first time in an eighth-century collection of laws. Thus its antiquity is respectable, if not venerable. But the underlying idea is far older, and the metaphor used carries us back to an ancient order of things.

It is plausibly supposed that the 'Book of Life' was a spiritual fancy corresponding to a quite material fact. We have several indications that at a fairly early date there was drawn up in Judea a civil list, or register, in which the names of fully qualified citizens were officially entered. Such a practice is attested by statements and allusions in Scripture, and it is probable that the figure of the 'Book of Life' was thence derived. To be enrolled in the Book of Life would imply membership of the divine commonwealth; to be blotted out would be to suffer disfranchisement.

From this image the step would be easy to a book containing a record of man's doings. This phase of the conception is found in the Mishnah. 'Know what is above thee – a seeing eye and a hearing ear, and all thy deeds written in a book' (Aboth. 2:1). These three things – which, as the author of the saying urges, restrain a man from sin – are in essence one, and they convey what is perhaps the leading principle of Judaism as a discipline. Individual responsibility, with the corollary of inevitable retribution; inevitable, that is, unless the wayfarer will divert himself to the road of repentance, prayer, and charity – the path by which the sinner finds a new approach to virtue and life. The moral is enforced in the third chapter of the same collection of 'Sayings of the Jewish Fathers,' where life is compared to a shop with its open ledger of credit and debit. Here, again, the idea is in germ scriptural. Sin blots man out from the book, virtue sets his name there in indelible ink ...

Some modern Jews are apt to feel a natural but unjustifiable repugnance to the notion of an annual balancing of the Book of Life. Certainly, the notion is sometimes presented crudely in the liturgy of the New Year and the Day of Atonement. Written in the Book of Life on the New Year, the entry is sealed on the Day of Atonement. In even more detail, a well known *piyyut*, or liturgical poem, for the New Year reproduced the old Rabbinical notion of the three books: one for the thoroughly righteous, one for the thoroughly wicked, and one for the intermediate class who, neither righteous nor wicked overmuch, can exchange hell for heaven by the blessed trilogy of repentance and prayer and charity. All this, if too mechanically expressed, is likely to be injurious. But when the Rabbis, with Abbahu in the Talmud, represented God as sealed at the New Year on the throne of judgment, with the books of the living and the books of the dead open before Him, all that they meant was to impart a stronger sense of gravity and a more than usual seriousness to the thoughts of men during the ten penitential days. Were they untrue to human nature in so doing? They understood better than we moderns that there is a time for everything; that man's conscience cannot bear the strain of continuous high pressure; that it is well for him to appoint a season for self-communion, a season when he can live morally and spiritually on a higher plane. 'The Rabbis were far from confining the need or utility of repentance to the penitential season from New Year to the Day of Atonement. Very common with them is the saying, "Repent one day before thy death." When his disciples said to R. Eleazar, "Does then a man know when he will die?" he answered, "The more necessary that he should repent to-day; then, if he die to-morrow, all his days will have been passed in penitence, as it says: Let thy garments be always white (Eccles. ix, 8)".' The annual stock-taking of a business man does not imply that he is a careless trader during the rest of the year. And the metaphor holds in the spiritual world also.[7]

FAITH AND WORKS

The Rabbinic religion knows nothing of any opposition between faith and works. The difficulties and problems which are raised by Paul in the Epistle to the Galatians and to the Romans were unfelt by them and would hardly have been understood. As we have seen, the Law, so far from being a burden, was a joy. So far from being an incitement or stimulus to sin – by awaking a desire the satisfaction of which it forbade – the Law was regarded as a medicine which prevented such desires from becoming masterful and overpowering. It was never doubted that man could, as he ought to, fulfil – up to a point – the laws of God, laws which would not have been given to him, if the power had not also been given to him to fulfil them. To order men to fulfil laws which they cannot fulfil would have been cruel. But God was not cruel, but merciful. He gave the Law, not to show its futility, but its usefulness, its beauty, and its joy. It is true that man often fails to fulfil it – he often sins; but such sins are inseparable from the very constitution of a being who is set between the animal and the angel: half earthly and half divine. There would be no discipline and no joy (to say nothing of no merit!) in fulfilment if to fulfil were inevitable. There would be no educative obedience if there were not the possibility of disobedience. In spite of occasional complaints about the power of the evil *Yetzer*, [inclination] there was no feeling of despair. The cry, 'Who shall deliver me from the body of death?' is, on the whole, an un-Rabbinic cry. The Rabbis won their way to God on their own lines. And with their strong, but rarely unethical, belief in God's mercy and forgiveness, they were not daunted by failure and lapses. The Law remained medicine and joy, and not burden and poison. Indeed (but this, perhaps, was a direct polemic against Paul, and therefore less interesting), they wanted the desire to be felt in order that the Law should be the more purely and powerfully fulfilled. To abstain from eating the pig or from unchasticy, what virtue and glory in that? But to abstain because the commandment bids you abstain, this is the right fulfilment of the Law and true service to God. The paradox is obvious – but no less obvious is its spirit. And just as there was little trouble as regards the Law because of human frailty, so there was little trouble because of any conflict between works with faith. There are few and rare indications in the Rabbinic literature of any theoretic unbelief, whether in the existence or in the power of God. It was needless to say: 'believe,' because all the Rabbis did believe and no suffering made them sceptical. Belief or trust in God was as natural to the Rabbis as belief in the regularity of night following day. And faith in the sense of making the Law in any of its parts superfluous would have seemed absurd or unintelligible. This seems to be the reason why the references to faith occur with such comparative infrequency ... the Rabbis were quite alert to its virtues, but they largely took it for granted: they did not theorise it, or dogmatise about it, and it would have greatly surprised them if they had been made to understand that the faith of Abraham, which they praised no less than the great antagonist, could actually be placed in opposition to the works of the Law.[8]

JEWISH ETHICS

Neither Biblical nor Rabbinic Hebrew has a word for ethics. A small tractate in the Mishnah often referred to as 'The Ethics of the Fathers', because it contains much ethical instruction, is entitled in Hebrew merely 'The Chapters of the Fathers'. Ethics is not conceived apart from religion, so that it is included in whatever expression, or expressions, Bible and Talmud use for religion. It belongs to the 'way of life' which Judaism prescribes to accord with 'the fear of the Lord'. Ethical injunctions with authority were just 'commandments of his Law' ...

Though the meaning of *torah* is obscured when it is translated by 'the Law', I shall for the sake of simplicity use that term for the revelation basically embodied in the Bible and Talmud but not wholly confined to, or comprised in, their literal statements. When, therefore, I assert that Jewish ethics is based on the Law, I mean that the ethical demands of Judaism derive their authority from the belief that they belong to divine revelation. Jewish ethics is rooted in the idea of divine law; and like divine law, it is concerned with the duties of men and their rights.

The belief that the Law contains the revelation of God was based on the story in Exodus of the theophany at Sinai. What historic fact lies behind the story need not concern us in our present study. Its theological significance, however, has relevance to the theory of Jewish ethics. It expressed, or embodied, the belief that the instruction which had come down from the past originated in a revelation from God. With it went the tradition that Moses was the channel of the revelation, the prophet through whom God transmitted it, so that all laws developed in the Jewish religion were ascribed to him, or traced back to words in the Pentateuch which was the recognized literary depository of the revelation he received.

Behind this particular belief about Moses lies the general belief that some men were inspired by God, so that they were his prophets, his spokesmen, entrusted with the knowledge of him and his commandments. All the prophets claimed that what they said came from God. Their consciousness of divine inspiration, and the consequent sense of an urgent mission, originated in a kind of mystical experience, which, though it varied in form with individuals, had this characteristic common to all the prophets, that it impressed them with the reality of God and with the realization of his righteousness and its working in the moral order of the universe. It was an immediate apprehension of God and his moral attributes ...

Whether or not the prophets' claim to inspiration be accepted as evidence that they were inspired, the fact remains that they proclaimed ideas which were new, and even startling, in their time, and which the later development of human thought has established so firmly as to make them common-place elements, though not always observed, in the faith and morals of western civilization. And it is a fundamental affirmation of theism that truth and righteousness have their source in God. Judaism makes that affirmation in its belief about the Law.

The conception of revelation which emerges from the relation between Talmud and Bible suggests its progressive character, and even implies that there is an element of relativity in its detailed results. '*Torah* connotes the whole body of Jewish teaching, legislation, practices, and traditions which have developed from the interpretation and re-interpretation of the laws of the Bible, to bring them into accord with reason, and the principles of righteousness, justice, and equity; as well as any adaptations or modifications made by spiritual leaders to meet changed conditions of life, economic, domestic and social.' That the Talmudic law represents a development was explicitly stated in the Rabbinic saying that 'Things not revealed to Moses were revealed to Rabbi Akiba'. Though ideas and laws in the Talmud are attached to the Bible, the connections are often so artificial that they must appear like afterthoughts. So the Mishnah says of some of the Talmudic laws that they 'have naught to support them' but 'are as mountains hanging by a hair'. Moreover, the rules by which these laws were given a Biblical basis were rejected by some Rabbis. In other words, the practices given Biblical authority in this way must have existed, or been developed, in their own right. That fact does not involve any judgement on their importance or on their divine character; it is still open to those who believe that they belong to a divine revelation to maintain that belief. It does however imply that there is a human element in the historic corpus of revelation.

Two Talmudic sayings must be quoted to support that conclusion. The schools (i.e., disciples continuing long after the death of their masters) of Hillel and Shammai held opposing views on many matters; yet it is said that the opinions of both were 'the words of the living God'. The apparent logical paradox is resolved by the conception of revelation which makes human reason its instrument – human reason, that is, stimulated and guided by devotion to God. That conception comes out with almost explicit clarity in another quotation: 'The views of the wise men in every generation are like the laws of Moses'; in other words, they have the quality of revelation. In conformity with this comprehensive view of revelation, the authority of divine inspiration was ascribed to some Rabbis. Because of their spiritual and moral attainment, it was said that they were worthy that the spirit of God should rest upon them.[9]

MORAL FREEDOM

Man's moral freedom is explicitly affirmed both in the Bible and Talmud. The Jewish doctrine is summed up in Ben Sirach's: 'God made man in the beginning, and left him in the hands of his own decision.' In the Bible, man's freedom is assumed in the story about the Ten Commandments, when the people voluntarily declare 'we will do and obey'; in the thirtieth chapter of Deuteronomy, where they are told to choose between obedience and disobedience to the law, which had been put to them, and their respective consequences; and in Joshua 24 where, in the spirit of Deuteronomy if not by the same author, the people are admonished to decide whether or not they would serve the Lord.

The doctrine of man's moral freedom underlies the laws of the Pentateuch and the exhortations of the prophets. There are, however, hints of restrictions which men themselves impose on their freedom by choosing the wrong course. In that sense the statement must be interpreted that: 'God hardened the heart of Pharaoh.' Similarly when Jeremiah, despairing of the people's reformation, asks 'Can the leopard change its spots?' (Jeremiah 13:23), he means that the people have by practising wrong become ingrained with it. It does not, however, detract from men's moral freedom, much less deny it, that men can become enslaved by their own sinful conduct.

Rabbinic teaching affirms tersely the moral freedom of men:

'All is in the hands of God except the fear of God.' It goes so far in its valuation of man's moral freedom, that it asserts that a man is helped to exercise it even if he choose to do wrong. God decrees human fortunes and even the physical traits of men, but it is left to men themselves whether or not they live in accordance with his will. It may be worth noting that the doctrine implies a restriction in, or diminution of, God's power. Men's attitude to God is excluded from his sovereignty. He has put that limitation on himself. Surprisingly, divine omniscience is not correspondingly limited. 'All is foreseen but free will is given' is the Rabbinic doctrine. It would seem, at first sight, that if an act can be foretold, even before the occasion for it arises, it is determined ...

Not being philosophers, the prophets, lawgivers and Rabbis did not perceive that human free will poses a problem for a theistic conception of the universal order, or if they perceived the problem they were not disturbed by it. Being practical religious teachers, they were concerned with human responsibility under the rule of God. So they just affirmed both human responsibility and the rule of God, without attempting to reconcile them in thought. Whatever way be adopted by philosophy to ease, solve, or remove the problem posed for theism by ascribing freedom to men, ethics, dealing with the practical conduct of life, must affirm that freedom, and Judaism has always affirmed it emphatically. Jewish ethics, and religious teaching throughout, is directed by the fundamental belief that every man is, by his human endowment, 'sufficient to stand but free to fall'. It is for him to choose. And his ultimate destiny will grow out of his choice. He has in himself, in his human nature, the capacity to follow a way of life, which will establish his personal relation with God. Without denying, or obscuring, the drive to sin in some human instincts, Judaism affirms the inherent goodness of man. Sin violates his human nature. Righteousness fulfils it.

Questions about the authority and exercise of conscience do not arise within the historic framework of Jewish ethics. The Law in its concrete form, that is, as embodied in Bible and Talmud, possesses absolute authority; it is men's duty to study it, to interpret its precepts, and to apply them in their conduct. The idea that the Law is appropriate to, or fits, the nature of man makes its commandments correspond to the dictates of conscience (cf. Proverbs 20:27); the correspondence is also implied in the ideal that the Law shall be written in the hearts of men. The good inclination in the Rabbinic doctrine of man covers, in some measure, what we mean by conscience. The general idea may fairly be inferred from all Jewish ethical teaching that man has in his natural human endowment the capacity to distinguish between right and wrong and the sense that makes it his duty to pursue the right.

Does the Law, however, allow any scope for the exercise of the individual conscience in deciding what is right and what is wrong? Some things, like filial piety and philanthropy, while the general duties are commanded, are, in measure and in detail, left to the individual conscience. The Rabbinic phrase is 'entrusted to the heart'. It is for example 'left to the heart' to fulfil the commandment to 'rise before the hoary head'. In one case, involving a question of damages, it is said that the one sued is not liable in a human court but is liable in the heavenly court. He is morally answerable, though not legally.

Duties are left to the conscience, which cannot be enforced, or punished, by law. Conscience enters into ethics to enforce the righteousness that transcends legal enactments. But that does not answer the larger question whether the individual conscience may judge between right and wrong. It is not answered by the statement that a good deed is rewarded by an approving conscience and an evil deed punished by a disapproving conscience. The approval may simply come from obedience to an authority, and disapproval from disobedience. In historic Jewish ethics, conscience was given the function to enforce obedience to the Law.[10]

RELIGION AND ETHICS

Several corollaries, with a practical bearing on human conduct, follow from the theory of Jewish ethics, which bases the moral duties of men on God's revelation of his nature, and affirms that men must, by their free will, fulfil these duties to establish their relation with God.

The first corollary is that morality consists of absolute principles. 'God does not change'; the duties of men, corresponding to his attributes, have their ground in the moral order of the universe. The belief in the Law implies that absolute criteria distinguish right from wrong in human conduct. That does not completely exclude an element of relativity in human morals. On the verse in Genesis 6:9, that Noah was 'a righteous man and perfect in his generation', some Rabbinic commentators stress the 'in his generation'. He was relatively righteous. I think it may be fairly said that Jewish ethics has allowed for relativity in moral judgement. The high responsibility laid on the people of Israel illustrates it. They were given the revelation of God, therefore more is demanded of them. So Amos declared, in what was probably his first sermon, that Israel will be punished for its moral shortcomings more than the other nations will be punished for theirs.

Though moral principles are absolute, emanating from God who does not change, men's apprehension of them changes with developments in human thought, life and moral sensitivity. It is fair that men's conduct be judged according to the apprehension they ought to have of moral principles. So the prophets judged their contemporaries severely for the failure to follow the developed religious instruction, with its ethical direction, which they brought under the inspiration from God. There may be a hint of relativity in religious beliefs generally in Malachi 1:11: 'For from the rising of the sun even unto the going down of the same my name is great among the nations; and in every place incense is offered unto my name, and a pure offering; for my name is great among the nations, saith the Lord of Hosts.' Some commentators put the verbs in the future tense, making the prophet express a Messianic hope; but with equally good reason, the verbs can be taken in the present tense. If so, the prophet allows variations in the worship of God. And permitted variations imply relativity …

The idea of relativity is expressed quite explicitly in the thought which the Rabbis ascribed to God: 'Not I in my higher realm but you with your human needs fix the form, the measure, the time and the mode of expression for that which is divine.' There is a further suggestion of relativity in the statement that the opposing views of the schools of Hillel and Shammai were both inspired. But relativity, whether in moral judgement or moral apprehension, does not conflict with the absoluteness of moral principles. Though they are absolute, their application in specific instances may be relative. They serve human life. There is no antithesis between absolute and pragmatic, divine and utilitarian, in the Jewish view of ethics. It is repeatedly said, and emphasized, that the Law was given that men may live by it ...

The second corollary from the theory of Jewish ethics is that ethical conduct is an integral part of piety. The pursuit of righteousness does not follow from religion, but is religion in practice. The distinction may entail a practical difference, but it certainly involves a theoretical difference. It is the difference between a dichotomy and a unity, the difference between religion *and* ethics and ethics *in* religion. The first implies that they can be separated; the second that they cannot be separated, except by such violence as will gravely impair both. It may be an open question whether in the general development of human thought morality began in religion; but certainly in the literary records of Judaism morality was from the earliest time emphatically included in religion. No exact date can be given for the promulgation of the Ten Commandments in their original – probably short – form, but they belong undoubtedly to a fairly early stage in the development of Judaism. Characteristically they begin with an affirmation about God, which is followed by laws (except the second commandment, which forbids idolatry) commanding morality in conduct and thought.

The oldest code of laws in the Bible, chapters twenty to twenty-three in Exodus, contains a mixture of legal provisions and moral precepts – all proclaimed in the name of religion. Many ethical injunctions in the Pentateuch conclude with the formula: 'I am the Lord thy God'. They belong to faith in him and the worship of him. The prophets define religion largely in ethical demands. Their religious judgements were guided by ethical considerations, their exhortations proclaimed ethical ideals. And the Book of Psalms, though mainly devoted to songs of faith, yet includes poems that define the way to God wholly in ethical terms (Psalms 15 and 24), and other poems which plainly imply (Psalm 1), where they do not state, the integration of ethics in religion. The large and important place given in the Bible to ethics has this general and fundamental significance: ethical duties belong to religion, being included in divine revelation. For Jewish ethics, therefore, morality is integrally bound up with religion. It belongs to the religious life; piety includes ethical conduct ...

Both religion and ethics are affected by the fundamental and integral relation between them. Three corollaries follow from it; of the first two, one is the converse of the other. The integration of ethics in religion raises conduct into the realm of the spirit and it brings the spirit into the realm of conduct.

1. It gives an ethical purpose to religious acts. The importance attached to religious observances made it highly meritorious to ransom Jews sold into slavery, so that they might fulfil them. The study of the Law has ethical implications – it means not only an intellectual pursuit but also practical instruction; its purpose is not only to learn what the Law teaches but also to follow its directions for moral conduct. Prayer, sin and repentance retain their primary spiritual meaning, but they have also an ethical connotation. It is a duty, according to Rabbinism, to pray for others. He who does not do so when he can is considered a sinner. Furthermore, prayer must include moral aspiration. Moral failures or lapses are sins, and repentance requires resolve to moral amendment. It is not only incomplete without such a resolve but also ineffective. The resolve must be fulfilled to make the penitence effective. If, as Maimonides says, it is not fulfilled when the occasion arises, then the penitence is nullified.

2. The second corollary from the integration of ethics in religion is that ethics must have an inward quality. Ethical conduct is infused with the spirit of piety. Ethics does not consist of an external code of injunctions for right conduct, but is an inward possession impelling and guiding to right conduct …

   The integration of ethical conduct into piety concerns not only the motives of acts but also affects their intrinsic quality. A good deed becomes a prayer. It contains a reference to God, with something like a mystical aroma. Some social acts, like the burial of the dead, have almost a ritual character. The thought of God is present in good deeds. Whosoever pleases (i.e. serves) men pleases God. A good deed is a pious act. It is a *Mitzvah*, a good deed, in fulfilment of a *mitzvah*, a commandment. These two senses of *mitzvah* bring out the intrinsically religious quality of ethical conduct; it has a God-ward intention. The religious, almost mystical, quality in ethical acts is derived from the general idea that righteousness brings men to God, that right conduct establishes their personal relation with him.

The place given to ethics in piety may explain why the little Talmudic book called *The Ethics of the Fathers* has been included in the traditional Prayer Book. At its best, Jewish ethical conduct has in it the spirit of worship. An act which fulfils the commandment 'Thou shalt love thy neighbour' is accompanied by the joyous feeling that it also fulfils the commandment: 'Thou shalt love the Lord thy God.' The two commandments go inseparably together.

3. In making ethical conduct essential to piety, Judaism raises the demands of ethics. This is the third corollary from the integration of ethics in religion. God expects from men a higher morality than men expect from one another. The adherents of Judaism have certainly not always, and perhaps only rarely, attained to this higher standard of conduct; but those who have, prove the truth of the doctrine that ethics in religion imposes higher standards for conduct than ethics without religion.[11]

THE DECALOGUE AND JEWISH LITURGY

The restoration of the Ten Commandments to their place in the service of the synagogue is one of the most notable of recent reversions to the past. There are now several synagogues in London alone in which this charter of social and religious virtue is recited from the pulpit every week. The Talmud says: 'Of right they should read the Ten Words every day. For what reason do they not read them? On account of the cavilling of the heretics, so that they might not say: These only were given to Moses on Sinai.' How strangely the wheel turns round in human thought! The 'modern heretic', in the guise of the Higher Critic, often singles out the Decalogue as the very thing that he thinks was *not* given to Moses at all. I do not share this doubt, for I have never seen adequate reason for doubting the Mosaic date of the Decalogue.

Though the Ten Commandments were discharged from the liturgy, Rabbinical fancy retained them by the interesting and ingenious discovery that the Decalogue is embodied in the Shema. The details, are somewhat forced, but the main thought is natural and true. The whole Torah, so far as concerns its moral contents, can be evolved from almost any one of its characteristic passages. With regard to the liturgical use of the Decalogue, I hardly know what to infer from the fact that the Ten Words seem in the early Middle Ages to have been sometimes written on separate little scrolls. I saw one at Cairo, taken from the Geniza, and reference is made to such scrolls in the Responses of the Gaonim ...

An extensive liturgical use of the Decalogue was made by the *paetanim*, as in Kalir's *Kerobah* for the second day of Pentecost. This is a metrical commentary on the Ten Commandments, and a fine translation of parts of the hymn is given by Zunz. Of another type were the numerous *Azharoth*, which contained a summary of the 613 precepts into which the Pentateuchal commands were grouped. According to the Gaon Nachshon's enumeration there are actually 613 words in the Decalogue, but there was, apart from any such numerical motive, a natural desire to include the whole of the Law in the homilies for the Feast of Weeks. In the all-night service celebrated in some homes on the previous evening, a section from every Sedrah is read, and the motive is the same. According to one Midrash, the Decalogue was written on the two tables of stone with long intervals, which gave space for adding all the rest of the precepts. These fancies grew up luxuriantly. It was felt, for instance, that the stones on which such precious words were written could not have been of ordinary material, but, to say the least, were made of diamond. The chips cut out during the engraving were enough to enrich Moses for life. There is no doubt a homiletical meaning in Midrashim of this class, a meaning so clear that it is superfluous to offer any help to the reader. The Decalogue was a source of wealth and of life: it enriched mankind and gave it vitality.

Have the Ten Commandments become obsolete? Are not the great principles 'Love God', 'Love man', enough? Let me answer in the words of Miss Wordsworth, taken from her excellent little book on the Decalogue: 'No doubt, any one who truly loved God and loved his neighbour would abstain from the acts forbidden in these Commandments; but, on the other hand, how easy it is to profess religious feelings in the abstract and never to bring our acceptance of a general principle to bear on the particular instances at all?'

The Inquisition professed great 'love' for the souls of those whom it tortured ... In fact, of not one of the Commandments can it be said that a mere general profession of love to God and man can be substituted for it. The ingenuity which the human mind displays, the sophistries which it employs in order to make what is supposed to be expedient seem right, the delicate shading by which it veils a disgraceful or undutiful act, the artifices to which it condescends, the self-flatteries which it is capable of where conscience is concerned, can only be met by plain, simple, distinct laws with great principles behind them such as we meet with in the Ten Commandments. All honour, then, to those who strove in the past and strive in the present to make the Decalogue a living force in the liturgy of the synagogue.

A reference has been made, or rather a hint given, to certain modern controversies regarding the re-introduction of the Decalogue into the regular liturgy. In all these matters, however, controversy has a way of softening with time into forbearance. And, in a very similar case, the Middle Ages supply a splendid instance of mutual toleration. The Jewish traveller, Benjamin of Tudela, visited Egypt in the latter part of the twelfth century, and he reports as follows: 'Here are two synagogues, one of the congregation of Palestine, called the Syrian, the other of the Babylonian Jews. They follow different customs regarding the division of the Pentateuch into *parashioth* and *sedarim*. The Babylonians read one *parasha* every week, as is the custom throughout Spain, and finish the whole of the Pentateuch every year (annual cycle). But the Syrians have the custom of dividing every *parasha* into three *sedarim*, thus completing the reading of the whole Pentateuch once in three years (triennial cycle).' And now note what follows. Despite this important liturgical difference, says Benjamin, 'they uphold, however, the long-established custom to unite the two congregations and to pray together on the Rejoicing of the Law, and on the feast of Pentecost, the day of the Giving of the Law'.

We should be the better nowadays for something of this medieval tolerance. 'The law which Moses commanded unto us is a heritage of the congregation of Israel.' Jew may differ from Jew, but on two days in the year Jew and Jew may and must unite. Brother must rejoice with brother in the Law; brother must stand by brother while the Decalogue is again read on the day associated with memories of Sinai.[12]

JEWISH TRAVELLERS IN MEDIEVAL TIMES

Before leaving home, a Jewish wayfarer of the Middle Ages was bound to procure two kinds of passport. In no country in those days was freedom of motion allowed to anyone. The Jew was simply a little more hampered than others. In England, the Jew paid a feudal fine before he might cross the seas. In Spain, the system of exactions was very complete. No Jew could change his residence without a licence even within his own town. But in addition to the inflictions of the Government, the Jews enacted voluntary laws of their own, forcing their brethren to obtain a congregational permit before starting.

The reasons for this restriction were simple. In the first place, no Jew could be allowed to depart at will, and leave the whole burden of the royal taxes on the shoulders of those who were left behind. Hence, in many parts of Europe and Asia, no Jew could leave without the express consent of the congregation. Even when he received the consent, it was usually on the understanding that he would continue, in his absence, to pay his share of the communal dues. Sometimes even women were included in this law, as, for instance, if the daughter of a resident Jew married and settled elsewhere, she was forced to contribute to the taxes of her native town a sum proportionate to her dowry, unless she emigrated to Palestine, in which case she was free. A further cause why Jews placed restrictions on free movement was moral and commercial. Announcements had to be made in the synagogue informing the congregation that so-and-so was on the point of departure, and anyone with claims against him could obtain satisfaction. No clandestine or unauthorized departure was permissible. It must not be thought that these communal licences were of no service to the traveller. On the contrary, they often assured him a welcome in the next town, and in Persia were as good as a safe-conduct. No Mohammedan would have dared defy the travelling order sealed by the Jewish Patriarch.

Having obtained his two licences, one from the Government and the other from the Synagogue, the traveller would have to consider his costume. 'Dress shabbily' was the general Jewish maxim for the tourist. How necessary this rule was may be seen from what happened to Rabbi Petachiah, who travelled from Prague to Nineveh, in 1175, or thereabouts. At Nineveh he fell sick, and the king's physicians attended him and pronounced his death certain. Now Petachiah had travelled in most costly attire, and in Persia the rule was that if a Jewish traveller died, the physicians took half his property. Petachiah saw through the real danger that threatened him, so he escaped from the perilous ministrations of the royal doctors, had himself carried across the Tigris on a raft, and soon recovered. Clearly, it was imprudent of a Jewish traveller to excite the rapacity of kings or bandits by wearing rich dresses. But it was also desirable for the Jew, if he could, to evade recognition as such altogether. Jewish opinion was very sensible on this head. It did not forbid a Jew disguising himself even as a priest of the Church, joining a caravan, and mumbling Latin hymns. In times of danger, he might, to save his life, don the turban and pass as a Moham-medan even in his home. Most remarkable concession of all, the Jewess on a journey might wear the dress of a man.

The law of the land was equally open to reason. In Spain, the Jew was allowed to discard his yellow badge while travel-ling; in Germany, he had the same privilege, but he had to pay a premium for it. In some parts, the Jewish community as a whole bought the right to travel and to discard the badge on journeys, paying a lump sum for the general privilege, and itself exacting a communal tax to defray the general cost. In Rome, the traveller was allowed to lodge for ten days before resuming his hated badge. But, curiously enough, the legal relaxation con-cerning the badge was not extended to the markets. The Jew made the medieval markets, yet he was treated as an unwel-come guest, a commodity to be taxed. This was especially so in Germany. In 1226, Bishop Lorenz, of Breslau, ordered Jews who passed through his domain to pay the same toll as slaves brought to market. The visiting Jew paid toll for everything; but he got part of his money back. He received a yellow badge, which he was forced to wear during his whole stay at the market, the finances of which he enriched, indirectly by his trade, and directly by his huge contributions to the local taxes.

The Jewish traveller mostly left his wife at home. In certain circumstances he could force her to go with him, as, for instance, if he had resolved to settle in Palestine. On the other hand, the wife could prevent her husband from leaving her during the first year after marriage. It also happened that families emigrated together. Mostly, however, the Jewess remained at home, and only rarely did she join even the pilgrimage to Jerusalem. This is a striking contrast to the Christian custom, for it was the Christian woman that was the most ardent pilgrim; in fact, pilgrimages to the Holy Land only became popular in Church circles because of the enthusiasm of Helena, mother of Constantine the Great, especially when, in 326, she found the true cross. We, however, read of an aged Jewess who made a pilgrimage to all the cities of Europe, for the purpose of praying in the synagogues on her route.

We now know, from the Chronicle of Achimaaz, that Jews visited Jerusalem in the tenth century. Aronius records a curious incident. Charles the Great, between the years 787 and 813, ordered a Jewish merchant, who often used to visit Palestine and bring precious and unknown commodities thence to the West, to hoax the Archbishop of Mainz, so as to lower the self-conceit of this vain dilettante. The Jew thereupon sold him a mouse at a high price, persuading him that it was a rare animal, which he had brought with him from Judea. Early in the eleventh century there was a fully organized Jewish community with a Beth-Din at Ramleh, some four hours' drive from Jaffa. But Jews did not visit Palestine in large numbers, until Saladin finally regained the Holy City for Mohammedan rule, towards the end of the twelfth century. From that time pilgrimages of Jews became more frequent; but the real influx of Jews into Palestine dates from 1492, when many of the Spanish exiles settled there, and formed the nucleus of the present Sephardic population.

On the whole, it may be said that in the Middle Ages the journey to Palestine was fraught with so much danger that it was gallantry that induced men to go mostly without their wives. And, generally speaking, the Jew going abroad to earn a living for his family, could not dream of allowing his wife to share the dangers and fatigues of the way ...

It is the traveller who can best discern, amid the ruins wrought by man, the hope of a divine rebuilding. Over the heavy hills of strife, he sees the coming dawn of peace. The world must still pass through much tribulation before the new Jerusalem shall arise, to enfold in its loving embrace all countries and all men. But the traveller, more than any other, hastens the good time. He overbridges seas, he draws nations nearer; he shows men that there are many ways of living and of loving. He teaches them to be tolerant; he humanizes them by presenting their brothers to them. The traveller it is who prepares a way in the wilderness, who makes straight in the desert a highway for the Lord.[13]

JEWS AND JUDAISM IN THE SEVENTEENTH CENTURY

Said to have been composed at the request of an English noble-man for the delectation of James I, Leon Modena's account of Jewish ceremonial was certainly intended for Christian readers. Though written in Italian, it first appeared in France (Paris, 1637), through the good offices of the author's pupil and friend, J. Gaffarel. It was the source of a whole library of similar books. Not only was it translated into several languages, but onwards from Modena's time, writers, Jewish and Christian, competent and incompetent, devoted themselves to the task of presenting to the world in general the teachings and customs of Judaism. The recent treatise of Oesterley and Box[14] is a lineal descendant of Modena's *Rites.*

Modena's own original was not, as the title suggests, a history. It does not so much give sources as facts. But this circumstance, that it is mainly *descriptive,* confers on it a permanent value. For it thus becomes a document. It helps us to realize several aspects of the Jewish position at the beginning of the seventeenth century. The author uses the term *history* in the sense of narrative; as he states in his Prefatory Epistle, he is concerned with the *what* and not with the *why* ('*Quod sunt*', not '*Propter quod sunt*', as he expresses it). He deals with his present, not with the past, and for that very limitation we may be grateful. He claims, too, that he is a 'Relater', not a 'Defender'. That being so, it is of peculiar interest to find what we do in his work, arranged in five books, 'according to the number of the Books of the Law.

Several forms of prayer appear for the first time in his pages. Certainly Chilmead is the earliest to give us in English the Prayer for the Government, or a translation of the Thirteen Articles drawn up by Maimonides. Modena, again, tells us that in his day it was customary to 'leave about a yard square of the wall of the house unplaistered on which they write either the verse of Psalm 137, "If I forget thee, O Jerusalem", or the words *Zecher Lahorban* – a Memorial of the Desolation.' He knows only *wooden*

Mezuzahs. Jews in Italy have pictures and images in their houses, 'especially if they be not with Relief, or Imbossed work, nor the Bodies at large'. Few, he reports, take heed to the custom of placing the beds north and south; many attach significance to dreams. Jewish men never paint their faces, for the custom is effeminate'; and 'in whatsoever country they are, they (the men) usually affect the long garment, or Gown'. The women dress 'in the habite of the countries where they inhabite'; but after marriage wear a *perruke* to cover their natural hair.

The Jews build their synagogues wherever they can, 'it being impossible for them now to erect any statelie or sumptuous Fabricks'. Things, as we know, soon after Modena's time became different, for by the middle of the seventeenth century, several fine synagogues were built in Rome and elsewhere. The women 'see whatever is done in the *School* (thus Chilmead renders *scuola* or synagogue), though they are themselves unseen of any man'. In the same city there will be places of worship 'according to the different customes of the Levantines, Dutch (German), and Italians'. Then, 'in their singing, the Dutch far exceed all the rest: the Levantines and Spaniards use a certain singing tone, much after the Turkish manner; and the Italians affect a more plain, and quiet way in their devotions'. The 'Favours of having a hand' in the acts connected with the reading of the Law 'are bought of the Chaunter, and he that biddeth most, shall have a share in them'.

Willingly, did space permit, we would follow the author through his account of the Judaism of his time. The majority of Jews, he says, are poor, yet annually they send 'Almes to Jerusalem, Safed, Tiberias, and Hebron'. The Jews never 'torment, or abuse, or put to any cruel death, any Brute Beast'. Very few Jews are able to speak Hebrew; all learn the language of the countries where they are born. 'Only those of the Morea still retain the Hebrew Tongue also, and use it in their Familiar Letters.' In Italy, he records, the Talmud continues utterly prohibited, and copies are not to be found in the country. Jews do not regard 'Vowes' as 'commendable'; yet 'when they are made, they ought to be kept'. Not many now observe the 'tradition' against eating 'Fish and Flesh together'. He tells us of an arrangement by which, for the Sabbath, some 'so ordered the matter aforehand, that the Fire should kindle itself at such and such a time'. The Passover bread is made in 'flat cakes of divers forms and shapes'. The 'Ceremonie with a Cock', on the eve of the Day of Atonement, 'is now left off both in the East and in Italy, as being a thing both Superstitious and Groundlesse'. But they still, on Purim, as often as they hear Haman named, beat the ground, and make a great murmuring noise. Bigamy 'is seldome or never used'. Marriages are usually performed before full moon, and the favourite days are Wednesdays and Fridays, with Thursdays for widows. 'Little boyes, with lighted torches in their hands' sing before the bridal couple, who are seated under the canopy. The Ketubah is read at the marriage. Modena mentions the charms against *Lilit*, and name-changing in case of sickness. He describes how, in Germany, in the case of girls, 'the Chaunter goeth home to the Parents house, and lifting the child's cradle on high, he blesseth it, and so giveth it the Name'. Modena also informs us that the Karaites were, in his time, numerous in Constantinople, Cairo, and Russia.

Modena records that among the Jews 'there are many women that are much more devout and pious than the men, and who not only endeavour to bring up their children in all manner of Vertuous Education; but are a means also of restraining their husbands from their Vitious Courses, they would otherwise take, and of inclining them to a more Godly way of Life'. With which handsome and just compliment we will take leave of our author.[15]

NOTES

1. Israel Mattuck, *Jewish Ethics*, London: Hutchinson (1953), pp. 142–5.
2. Claude Montefiore (with Herbert Loewe), *A Rabbinic Anthology*, London: Macmillan (1938), pp. xxiii–xxv.
3. Claude Montefiore, *The Old Testament and After*, London: Macmillan (1923), pp. 299–300.
4. Israel Abrahams, *Studies in Pharisaism and the Gospels*, Cambridge: Cambridge University Press (1924), pp. 73–80.
5. Claude Montefiore, 'A Few Rabbinic Ideals', unpublished sermon, 1930, in LJS archives, Box 95, pp. 4–6.
6. Montefiore, *The Old Testament and After*, pp. 140–2.
7. Israel Abrahams, *Festival Studies*, London: Macmillan, pp. 19–23.
8. Montefiore, *The Old Testament and After*, pp. 384–5.
9. Mattuck, *Jewish Ethics*, pp. 19–23.
10. Ibid., pp. 36–40.

11. Ibid., pp. 41–50.
12. Abrahams, *Festival Studies*, pp. 88–90.
13. Israel Abrahams, *A Book of Delight*, Philadelphia: JPS, pp. 123–57.
14. W. Oesterley and G. Box, *The Religion and Worship of the Synagogue: An Introduction to the Study of Judaism from the New Testament Period*, London: Sir Isaac Pitman and Sons (1911).
15. Israel Abrahams, *By-Paths in Hebraic Bookland*, Philadelphia: JPS, pp. 136–43.

5

Liberal Judaism

THE AGENDA OF LIBERAL JUDAISM

Large and important is the work which Liberal Judaism has accomplished. If we recognise that its own edges are still rough, though less rough than the edges of the Old Testament, we yet believe that it is capable of smoothing them. Much we can see which remains to be done; much doubtless will be done which we cannot see. That which remains and which we can see is mainly to complete what has already been achieved, and to do so on the same lines. We have gradually to let our ideas shine forth more perfectly from our institutions, to let our forms reflect our doctrines more completely. That must be a long and difficult task, in which it is better to go too slow than too fast. It is not easy, though sometimes the attempt may have to be made, to retrace a false, or even an inexpedient step. We may, however, be fairly satisfied with the work, all imperfect though it may be which has already been achieved. Liberal Judaism has taken up again, on distinctive Jewish lines, the teachings of the Prophets. It has, we may truly say, put Prophets and Law in a new position and relation to each other. It has religiously emancipated women, and in this respect, as in some other respects, it has become a religion suited to, and fitted for, the western world. It has attempted to denationalise Judaism and to universalise it. It has fashioned or adopted new ideas of much moment and significance concerning revelation and inspiration, as well as new ideas concerning authority and freedom. It has boldly and openly faced the new conclusions of history and criticism, and sought to find new adjustments to them. It has attempted to fashion a Judaism which can look Science in the face without flinching, which is independent of the dates and authorships of the Biblical books and of the miracles recorded in them. It has sought to free Judaism from absolute priestly conceptions.

It has abandoned the Talmudic theory of the *ukas* [Edicts] as applied to the ceremonial enactments of the Pentateuchal Code, a theory which, while, as must be gladly admitted, it largely got rid of superstition, yet rested upon the hypothesis that, for various good reasons, the perfectly wise and perfectly good God had directly ordained and commanded all these enactments, whether one could find parallels for them in many other races in certain stages of civilisation or not. Liberal Judaism has deliberately restricted the idea of religious purity and impurity of states of the soul, in other words, to virtue and to sin. Physical ailments and bodily conditions are, religiously, neither pure nor impure, and the physically clean is to be distinguished from the religiously clean: in other words, ritual cleanness or uncleanness is abolished. Yet Liberal Judaism no less than Traditional Judaism, and with greater success and efficacy for the modern world, seeks to make religion coterminous with life. It gives to cleanliness – even physical cleanliness – a religious value, but a value very different from the priestly ideas of cleanliness which have hitherto prevailed. Liberal Judaism seeks to fashion a Judaism which shall be broad enough and humble enough to believe that its own truths, its own treasures, can be enriched and added to from the truths and treasures which may have been vouchsafed to other than Jewish teachers. It does not attempt to fashion a Judaism which shall be a mere medley of pretty notions gathered from every source. But it attempts to make its own doctrines still richer and fuller, and no less harmonious and consistent, by selected garnerings from without. One set of garnerings, however, can hardly be rightly held to come from without. So far as we can learn from Jesus and even from Paul, we learn from Jews, and not from aliens. While Liberal Judaism must not hesitate to differ from these illustrious men, it need not hesitate also to learn from them. From their teaching, too, it may adopt and adapt what suits it, and what appears to it to be true. Free in respect of the Old Testament, it may claim a similar freedom as regards the New. Fearless it is and unperplexed 'what weapons to select, what armour to imbue'. So does it go forth into the battle of life, in hope and joy, trusting to truth and to God.[1]

TO BE A JEW

The history of the Jews is their life-story in which God has manifested Himself. It contains the revelation of God on the human plane.

Jewish history and the Jewish religion are, therefore, inter-woven. And this, incidentally, answers the people who ask why Jewish history is given a large place in the religious instruction of Jewish children. It is because Jewish history is a part of the Jewish religion. The study of it can, therefore, serve the religious life of the Jew in two ways. In the first place it can introduce him, so to speak, to God. Secondly, it can cultivate the Jewish consciousness, that is, the feeling in the individual Jew of his identity with the Jewish people. And an effective sense of membership in the community of Israel can help the individual to establish his personal relation with God. It brings him nearer to God and it brings God's law effectively into his life.

At the same time and for the same reason it can enforce a high sense of responsibility. The special relation between God and Israel entails a collective obligation on the Jews; they have a mission. Every Jew has an individual share in the obligation, which he can fulfil by living up to the highest spiritual and moral demands of Judaism. Because he is a Jew, he must, under the instruction of Judaism and in loyalty to the Jewish people, pursue in the name of God and Judaism the moral and spiritual ideals which constitute righteousness ...

From the definition of what it means to be a Jew we can deduce the ideal of the good Jew. It begins with faith. The good Jew must give to faith in God the commanding place in his life. The desk at which the leader of the Service stands in some synagogues has the inscription (in Hebrew): Know before whom thou standest. For the good Jew the admonition applies to the whole of life: Know before whom (in whose presence) thou livest. A great philosopher has said that we should look at things in the light of eternity. Similarly the good Jew must strive to live by the light of faith in God. With it he faces all that life brings him, thanking God for its blessings, drawing help from Him to bear its burdens, and resisting its blows with a spiritual power that turns them into spiritual progress.

Secondly, the good Jew must pursue righteousness. By his faith in God he is instructed in the knowledge of righteousness and impelled to live righteously, to exercise love and justice in all his relations with others, and to work for a social order based on justice and infused with the spirit of human brotherhood.

Thirdly, the good Jew must give time to prayer and study. In them he expresses, and by them he feeds, his faith in God, using his spiritual, intellectual and emotional endowments in His service.

Fourthly, the good Jew feels the solidarity of Israel. He identifies himself with the life of the Jewish people, realizing his obligation to help Jews who suffer special hardship because they are Jews, and, above all, realizing the responsibility which the mission of Israel lays on every Jew to show by his life the power of Judaism and to contribute by his life to its influence.

Fifthly, the good Jew must conceive life, personality, and conduct in terms of holiness. Observances can help him to keep the ideal before him and to give his life and home that indefinable atmosphere which we call the beauty of holiness. Though few among men have fully attained to holiness yet it belongs to the religious conception of life to strive for it. It distinguishes the religious from the nonreligious way of living. All that holiness means is included in the third element of Micah's definition of the good life: to walk humbly with God. It is the ideal for character and conduct, unattainable as it is majestic, but Judaism makes it the guide to the Jewish way of life.[2]

THE HEBREW BIBLE IS THE FOUNDATION OF LIBERAL JUDAISM

For Liberal Judaism, as we have already heard, has made the Law secondary and the Prophets primary; it has put ritual into its proper place; it has rejected priestly, primordial conceptions of clean and unclean; and while it has distinguished and disentangled the conception of Law from the actual Pentateuchal Code, it has sought to give to Law its right place in religion and in Judaism.

Corresponding to these immense changes in doctrine are the changes in form. We have maintained the festivals, but how different is our way of celebrating them, and how different are the conceptions which we put into them! Even the Sabbath is not quite the same for us as it was for the authors of the Pentateuchal codes. Greater still is the change as regards Passover and Pentecost, and greatest and most remarkable of all is the change in the greatest of all the festivals, the Day of Atonement. I have so often laid stress upon the gulf which separates the priestly ceremonies described in Leviticus 16 from the prophetic and spiritual Day of Atonement of our Liberal Judaism today that I need not dwell upon the matter further in this book. But what is no less to be emphasized is that the second is the lineal descendant of the first. The historic connection is unbroken.

This historic connection reminds us that, however great and significant the changes in Liberal Judaism from many of the doctrines, or even from the prevailing doctrines of the Old Testament may be, still more remarkable, perhaps, is the fact that Liberal Judaism still finds in the Old Testament both its spiritual ancestry and its nourishment. It may be that, as I have shown, we have made the secondary primary, and the primary secondary, that we have put what was occasional and sporadic into the forefront and into the centre. It may be that we have expanded and curtailed, modified and spiritualized. But our very inspiration to do all this has been, in some measure, the Old Testament itself. We have had Amos and Isaiah for our teachers; they have pointed out to us the way. There is hardly a conception or a doctrine of ours which does not go back, even if only in germ, to the Hebrew Bible. It is true that we have to abandon certain prevailing doctrines, but we do not abandon, we only expand and deepen, strengthen and confirm, the most fundamental doctrines of all. God's unity and righteousness, the inseparable union of religion and morality, the election of Israel for a religious mission and service, the joy of communion with God – these doctrines, the essence of our Judaism today, are all found in the pages of the Hebrew Bible. The supreme revelations of the Hebrew Bible constitute the core of our Judaism, the core of our own religion, the core, as we believe, of the future religion of all mankind. We, too, can say of this book, as the gentile proselytes are to say of Zion, 'All my fountains are in thee.'[3]

FREEDOM OF CHOICE

Only Liberal Judaism possesses liberty – conscious, reasoned and deliberate. Only Liberal Judaism has nothing to fear. Only Liberal Judaism can stand above the facts, and examine its own house reverently, tenderly, lovingly, but freely. For by the conception of progressive revelation, by the conception of the spirit of God giving light to all generations and to all mankind, so that no one religion, and no one stage of that religion, are in possession of perfect truth in all its fullness and completion only by these conceptions Liberal Judaism has won its power to smooth the 'rough edges', to fill the gaps, to strengthen the weak points and generally to expand and to modify, to adapt and to adopt, to curtail or to reject. It has won the power and the capacity to do this in happy freedom and in the full light of day. It is a grand and solemn power, a power to be made use of in all soberness and caution, in all reverence and care; it is a power in the exercise of which some mistakes are bound to be made, and some ephemeral conclusions to be drawn, but it is a power which, in spite of its dangers (and what high gift of God has not its dangers?) must yet be used, and in the use of which a distinctive feature, privilege and glory of Liberal Judaism are to be found. Liberal Judaism need not explain away: it need not turn molehills into mountains, or mountains into molehills. It need not regard the exceptional as usual, or the usual as exceptional. It need not make a single saying mean more than it really meant, or less. In a word, it can be honest, historical, and free. If it is to make the best use of its freedom, it must and dare not be anything but honest.

These new conceptions and this new freedom constitute a tremendous advance. They suffice to make Liberal Judaism, while preserving a true historic connection with all the phases of Judaism which have preceded it, yet enormously different from any of them. Neither Hebrew Bible nor Rabbinic Talmud is immaculate or complete in doctrine or institution, in morality or in religion. We distinguish between the divine and human elements in both these books, and we are not disconcerted because those very words 'divine and human elements' are a rough and inadequate expression for a truth too profound and subtle for our full and clear comprehension. They are, at any rate, more true than false; they serve. We distinguish between the impermanent and the permanent; between truths which appear to us eternal, and the transitory and imperfect expressions of those truths. We distinguish doctrines and institutions which we desire to maintain for their truth and their value from doctrines and institutions which we desire to put aside or to abolish; we distinguish between the living and the obsolete.

Expanding what has just been said a little, we may, perhaps, affirm that Liberal Judaism makes use of its freedom in four or five main directions or ways.

1. It modifies or enlarges the doctrines of the past – the doctrines which it inherits and finds – so as to make them consistent with each other and in harmony with the highest conceptions of truth to which it can attain. And some ancient doctrines may have to be dropped altogether, and some doctrines may have to be added. It further seeks to make the private and public institutions of religion the purest possible manifestations and expressions of its doctrine.

2. Liberal Judaism deliberately aims at universalism and universalisation, though the goal may be distant and the pathway long. It would not merely desire to possess and teach only such doctrines as may be fervently held by all races, and as are fully coexistent with the fundamental dogma of the One God who is the impartial father of all mankind, but it would desire that its religious rites and institutions should, as far as possible, harmonise with its universalist doctrines. It would wish to magnify and exalt the purely religious elements in Judaism, and to depreciate and minimise the purely national elements; it would wish, so far as practicable, gradually to disentangle the first from the second, and, so far as any national rites and institutions are retained, to clothe and suffuse them with new spiritual and universalist values and meanings.

3. Liberal Judaism sets out to emphasise the 'prophetic' elements in Judaism, and to minimise or negate the 'priestly' elements. Thus it abandons priestly conceptions of clean and unclean; it rejects the idea of 'holiness' as attaching to things as well as to persons in a real, serious, and outward sense; it gives up praying for the restoration of the Temple and of animal sacrifices.

4. Liberal Judaism tends to exalt the 'prophetic' elements in Judaism, and to depreciate, though not to abandon, the purely legal elements. It sets the Prophets above the Law. It desires to make Judaism no longer a predominantly legal religion,

though it does not desire to deny or ignore the place of Law and of the Law (i.e. the Pentateuch) in the Jewish religion as a whole.

5. Liberal Judaism seeks to construct a Judaism which is independent of the dates and authorships of the Biblical books, which is free to accept the assured conclusions and results of Biblical criticism, and which does not require any belief in the miracles of the Pentateuch.[4]

THE AUTHORITY OF TRADITIONAL LITERATURE

We recognise no binding outside authority between us and God, whether in man or in a book, whether in a church or in God, whether in a tradition or in a ritual. Most, if not all, of our differences from the traditionalists spring from this rejection of an authority which they unhesitatingly accept. The fact of our rejection of the supreme and binding authority of a book and a code is due to two causes which support and co-operate with each other. The first is philosophical; the second, historical. We cannot conceive the perfection of God enshrined in, or precipitated into, a book or code. A book or code is something human. However 'inspired' it may be, it must nevertheless possess its human limitations. It must have been written down by mortal hands, and have passed through human brains. It must bear the impress of time and locality, of race and environment. It cannot from the very nature of the case be perfect, for it must bear the stamp of the man or men by whom it was written – touched, even though they were by the spirit of God. We cannot curb and confine the infinite God within the paragraphs of a code. No book or code, therefore, can stand between us and God. We must bring our God-given reason to criticize, accept, or reject any human production, however much we may rightly say of such a 'human' production that it is also 'divine'. Thus, even before we open the Book, before we open the Code, we know that it cannot be for us an infallible and eternal authority. Even if the whole Pentateuch were unquestionably the work of Moses, we should still declare that no book, be its human author who it may, can be for us an unquestioned and binding authority.

To free ourselves from the heavy bondage of the Rabbinical law and of the Shulchan Aruch may be, and indeed is, desirable and necessary. But the bondage of the written law of the Pentateuch, or the view that the 'Bible, and the Bible alone,' is the religion of Judaism may be even heavier, or at all events more fossilising, than the Bible plus the interpretations and additions of Tradition. The written word remains: it is the same for all ages; it can never grow, expand, and develop. But we stand for the conception that religion is progressive. However much we owe to and draw from the past, we cannot be bound to it, or to a certain product of it, in the sense that we are to see exactly as it saw. Religion grows. The Judaism of today will, we trust, be found inferior in many things to the Judaism of two hundred years hence. Our descendants will profit from our thoughts and feelings and experience; they will advance upon them and beyond them. The idea of development, for which we stand, is inconsistent with the absolute authority and final perfection of a particular Book.

We, therefore, do not take up the attitude of the earlier Jewish reformers towards the Bible and Talmud. We do not allow the authoritative power to the former, and deny it to the latter. We recognise the Spirit of God in the Talmud as well as in the Bible. Though the second is a much greater 'book' than the first, it too has its human, just as the other has its divine, elements. For the Talmud also contains many good and true words, and what is good and true has its source in God. We cannot, therefore, allow any abstract and rigid separation between the Biblical and the Rabbinic codes.[5]

LIBERAL AND ORTHODOX JUDAISM

Several practical differences between Liberal and Orthodox Judaism follow from their divergent views of revelation. Bible and Talmud, since they embody for Orthodox Judaism a complete and perfect divine revelation, are its authority. They constitute the standards for the knowledge of truth, contain all the laws, which Jews must obey, and prescribe the practices, which they must observe. Those Jews who do not themselves know what is contained in these books, or who cannot understand them, must consult those who do know – authoritative teachers of the Law. Liberal Judaism, on the other hand, does not recognize any external authority. Bible and Talmud, valuable as they are, do not contain the final word about truth, righteousness and the worship of God. They are not the whole of Judaism. Though they contain a very large and supremely important part of God's revelation to the Jews, they cannot contain the whole of it.

Because Liberal Judaism maintains that revelation is progressive, it cannot recognize as final any set of ideas – enunciated in the past, or now. Moreover, each individual has the duty himself to strive for the instruction and guidance of God. He must, with his own spirit, try to learn what is required of him in the worship of God. The results of his own spiritual efforts must be correlated with the results of the best spiritual efforts of the present and past ages. All these together should produce the authoritative result, should reveal to the individual his duties, and teach him the knowledge of God.

Let it not, however, be supposed that by its conception of revelation, Liberal Judaism denies in any way the inspiration, in varying degrees, of our ancient teachers. Quite the contrary. But it recognizes that there is a human element in revelation, that God's instruction of man is regulated by man's capacity to receive it, that the revelation which came to each age was restricted by the capacities and limitations of that age.

The recognition of the human element in revelation solves many of the difficult problems connected with the Bible. Those who accept the Bible as a perfect and complete revelation, which was given to man without any consideration for man's limited capacities, may find it very hard to explain those things in it which to us seem very crude, the stories which we cannot believe, and the laws which seem unjust. With the belief in progressive revelation, the difficulty disappears. The human element in the Bible explains its limitations.

Because of their different conception of revelation, Orthodox and Liberal Judaism also differ in their attitude to ideas which have come into existence since the Bible and Talmud were produced. Orthodox Judaism cannot accept them if they contradict anything in the Bible or Talmud. Liberal Judaism can. 'Truth is God's seal,' said Rabbi in the Talmud. Whatever is true, therefore, has the quality of revelation. Orthodox Judaism, for example, cannot accept the idea of evolution because it seems to contradict the first chapter of Genesis. Liberal Judaism, on the other hand, can accept it as a later revelation, a further development in man's knowledge of truth.

In the same way there is a difference in the attitude to religious ceremonies. Those who accept the authority of tradition must consider themselves bound to observe all the practices which it commands, whether or not they have any particular present significance. On the other hand, those who do not accept the authority of tradition, even while recognizing its value, judge the religious practices which it has transmitted by their meaning for, and effect on, the spiritual and moral life of Jews today.

There is a common notion that the difference between Orthodox Judaism and Liberal Judaism is that Orthodox Jews observe certain things, and Liberal Jews do not. There are such differences between them. Liberal Judaism leaves personal observances, such as the dietary laws, to the religious conscience and thought of the individual Jew. Their value depends on their significance for, and effect on, the religious life of individuals. The same principle is applied by Liberal Judaism to the minutiae which Orthodox Judaism prescribes for the observance of holydays.

Some ceremonies, however, which Orthodox Judaism maintains with insistence on their obligatory character, Liberal Judaism has definitely abolished. One example is the ceremony called 'Chalitzah' which is described in Deuteronomy 25: 8–10. Another example is the special attention given in the Synagogue Services and in some ritual laws to those who claim to be descended from the priests who served in the Temple (in Hebrew, Cohanim; singular Cohen). But all the differences result from the fundamental difference in their conceptions of revelation.

Orthodox Judaism follows the past. Liberal Judaism bases itself on Jewish tradition, but it takes account of modern thought and considers the circumstances and religious needs of Jewish life in the present. Ultimately, the authority for the religious life is to be found in the spiritual experience of the individual, supported by the experience of his own age, and influenced by the religious experience of preceding ages.[6]

THE LAW IN LIBERAL AND ORTHODOX JUDAISM

To Orthodox Judaism the Law is primary, and the Prophets are secondary: secondary both in importance and date. To Liberal Judaism the great prophets (Amos, Hosea, Isaiah, Jeremiah) are primary: the Law is secondary; secondary both in importance and in date. This does not mean that the Law is not important at all. If there were two mountains, one of 15,000 feet and one of 12,000 feet, the second is lower than the first. But the second is also high. So it is with the Prophets and the Law in the scheme of Liberal Judaism. The Law is honoured; but the Prophets are honoured still more. Liberal Judaism recognises the place of Law in religion and of the Law in Judaism. But if Liberal Judaism is partly 'legal', it is yet more prophetic. It accepts as the deeper and greater portion of its faith, the famous utterances: 'I desire love and not sacrifice, and the knowledge of God rather than burnt offerings.' 'What does the Lord's command require of thee, but to do justice, and to love mercy, and to walk humbly with thy God.' It accepts them and draws the consequences.

Unlike Orthodox Judaism, it can, and it does, cheapen Leviticus 19:19: in comparison with Leviticus 19:18.[7] And I may even say that, as regards some details of the old ceremonial law, this cheapening is not merely comparative, but also positive – positive, at all events, in relation to our present knowledge and our present life. Liberal Judaism, for example, can perceive, and is able to recognise, the needlessness and pettiness of many Rabbinical prescriptions about the Sabbath or about food. It recognises that laws about food are world-wide, and common to innumerable races. It realises that these laws do not pertain to what was new and specific in Judaism, but to what was common to it and many other religions; that they belong not to what separated Judaism from endless pagan tribes, but to what united it to them; that they are not the creations of its prophets or even of its lawgivers, but old customs and taboos, adopted by the lawgivers and given a fresh religious sanction and reference.[8]

SANCTIFICATION OF THE SABBATH

We are no less eager to sanctify the Sabbath than our Orthodox brothers and sisters, but we feel that the sanctification must be effected in a living way, though also at the cost of sacrifice. We can no longer just refer to the paragraphs of a code. We ask that every Liberal Jew should himself consider whether a given action is or is not consistent with Sabbath sanctification, with making the Sabbath a day of peace and joy, different from other days to some extent even in its pleasures. Two questions have to be put. First, is a given pleasure (for example) in accordance with the spirit of the Sabbath? The reply might condemn such pleasures as card-playing, visiting cinemas or races. Secondly, is a certain pleasure or action undesirable on Saturday for me? If my circumstances never enable me to play cricket except on Saturday, that is a good reason for playing cricket on Saturday. If my circumstances (of which I take advantage) enable me to play cricket on other days, that is a good reason for abstaining on Saturday. The mind must be used in these matters, not a mere rule of thumb. Then as to work. Orthodox Judaism seldom seems to be able to preach a higher point of view. To work on the Sabbath is a sin, be the consequences of abstention what they may. So many an Orthodox Jew works on Saturday because economic pressure compels him, but he says that it is a sin. The result is often unfortunate. What you continue habitually to do, while you yet regard it as a sin, becomes in the end no sin. The sin is acknowledged with the lips in a purely formal manner. Religion gradually drops out of the man's real life and out of his heart. Liberal Judaism says definitely: to work on the Sabbath because of economic pressure is no sin. Your relation with God can remain as good and pure as before. But all the more important does it make it become how you use the hours on Friday evening and of Saturday when you are free. And the ideal of Liberal Judaism is hard and severe. If you have a few free hours on the Sabbath, all the more careful should you be how you employ them. If a suitable service is arranged on Saturday afternoons for those who work on Saturday mornings, it is really a misuse of words to say that we ask the Sabbath workers to come to this service because it is held at a convenient hour. It is held at a possible hour, if you like, but, we would be quite open and frank, not necessarily by any means for all persons at a convenient hour. I wish I could think so! Then on Saturday afternoon services would be fuller than they are! For Liberal Judaism demands sacrifice: in this case the sacrifice (and this is hard) of some leisure and quiet. But we believe in public worship; we believe in the religious advantage and utility of congregational prayer. And so we ask the Jew who works on Saturdays to make a sacrifice of his hard-earned leisure, and to acquire the taste and habit of worship. We will provide the service, if he will come to it, if he will sacrifice his convenience, make the effort to come. 'No suitable service' is the excuse which just suits the man who has to work on Saturdays and does not want to sacrifice his convenience.[9]

SABBATH OBSERVANCE

We Liberal Jews think that the Sabbath is of benefit to all mankind, and it is for this reason that it has been generally accepted. Through its intrinsic merits it makes its claim on universal acceptance ...

Our methods of observing the Sabbath vary according to the religious outlook which we accept. Our ancient Rabbis, believing the Sabbath to be directly ordained by God, felt that it must be accepted for all time, and in order to prevent any laxity in observance, made a fence round the law. With the greatest care they framed their injunctions, and men were not only forbidden to work on the Sabbath, but to do anything which involved the labour of others, such as traveling or recreation. They were not allowed to risk any form of destruction; they must not play instrumental music lest they break their instrument, or open their letters, for this was a manner of work. Liberal Jews regard the Sabbath as valuable in festering their spiritual life. They, like their Orthodox co-religionists, should attend public worship on the Sabbath for in this way Jewish fellowship is nurtured. They should abstain from work even if this abstention involves sacrifice so long as it is economically possible. If the choice is between Sabbath work and being a burden on the community, it is, we think, man's duty to work for his independent maintenance, and so long as his work is honourable, he can pass from his workshop or office to his Synagogue, and remain all the while in the house of God. But he must not think it unimportant to hallow, as far as possible, the Sabbath through worship ...

It is of value to us to remember that this observance has been ordered all through the ages, generation by generation. *Of course* we can pray at home just as well as in Synagogue, but we *do* derive help and guidance from the addresses given by our Ministers and from the readings from the Bible. Throughout the ages the Sabbath has been a day for rejoicing and worship, and rest and instruction. If our Service is in harmony with our actual needs and completely understood by us all, we can through its help not only feel the influence of the past, but be stirred also to make our own contacts with the living God.

There is a tendency today to make the Sabbath just another day on which we lead a secular life, even if through the reorganization of work, a five day week for business can be instituted. People do not seriously consider the Sabbath as a means for the sanctification of life. Our spiritual growth is impeded, and our portion of aesthetic and cultural education is diminished through neglect. The hours for rejoicing on the Sabbath Day must not be neglected even though the time for rest and worship and study is given its due recognition. We Liberals consider the authority for observance to rest in the trained conscience of the individual, who is guided by the teaching of great scholars, and also by his own communion with God, the loving guide of all men. The appeal is to every man who would use Jewish teaching for the sanctification of his life, in conformity with his highest conception, to ask himself how far certain forms of sociability, or recreation develops his cultural, aesthetic, and spiritual well-being, and how far they may impede it. In the light of these questions he tries to order his life.

There is one part of the Sabbath which Orthodox, Conservative, Reform and Liberal adherents hold to be of the greatest possible importance, and that is the Sabbath Eve. All Jewish holydays and festivals have their beginning in the evening. New birth is always shrouded in the mystery of darkness. We welcome the Sabbath Eve. It comes as a messenger from the past to sanctify family joy and to consecrate the home. The purity of family life has always been one of the glories of our community, and it owes much to the observance of the Sabbath Eve as holy. The symbols are beautiful and suggestive. The two candles are generally lighted by the mother who, through this symbol, asks that all small quarrels and jealousies be cleared away by the flame of the Lord, which at the same time is an emblem of purity. Joy is sanctified with the blessing of the wine in the Kiddush Cup. Thanksgiving for the gifts of the earth is spoken by means of the blessing on the two loaves. The cup of wine is passed round to express family unity. The work and distractions of the week have perhaps kept the members of the family separate, but on the Sabbath they come together, and laugh and eat together after family worship, and also talk over family affairs. The opportunity is given and appreciated by parents and children who have been accustomed to regard the Sabbath as an institution deserving of faithful, inflexible observance. It can only be of value if it can claim absolute loyalty. If the members of the family can only be counted upon to remain at home if no other engagement offers itself, it is of little or no value.[9]

BELONGING TO A SYNAGOGUE

Human beings do work most effectively through groups, and the platform from which we bear our testimony is, of course, our Synagogue. I wonder how many people regard their Synagogue as a useful centre for the holding of public worship which we like to think goes on from week to week, much in the same way, and which we may attend when it is convenient for us to do so, when the weather is propitious and we feel on the whole inclined for it. It is also a place where our children can receive religious education and where marriage and burial ceremonies are performed when required. Is that not all which a number of us Jews ask of our Synagogue? When we attend, we criticize the sermons, favourably or unfavourably; we say whether we think the building is too hot or too cold; we express our views on the strength or weakness of the choir; but membership in a Liberal Synagogue should not be of this kind. By belonging to a Synagogue, we stand for a certain presentment of Judaism which affords us spiritual stimulus and guidance. The authority for our religious conceptions is no longer to be found in a perfect code, verbally true, but in the trained conscience of the individual who has reverently studied the past teaching and for himself sought enlightenment in prayer and meditation.

Our Synagogues form part of a Union which exists to spread and to perpetuate this particular form of Judaism, because we believe that it contains within itself a guidance to right living in harmony with the conditions under which we live, and the knowledge acquired by the human intelligence working from the beginning down to the present day.

What do you give to your Synagogue? Of course, I know you pay your subscription and are ready to contribute money to every special need which arises. But important though that material assistance is, we ask for an infinitely more worthwhile contribution. We ask for some of yourself, some of your thoughts and emotions, the expression of your beliefs and aspirations. The Synagogue is meant to influence life. It supplies us with a spiritual outlook on the affairs and opinions of every day, on the well-being of our city, our country, and in fact the whole world. Many activities of social value should emanate from the Synagogue. By that I do not mean that we should all be engaged in social service with a capital S. Some people are not fashioned that way, and their efforts would be unacceptable to those they desire to serve. They lack the particular form of imaginative sympathy necessary for such work, but they can, nevertheless, be socially minded and in their homes and in their business and in their recreation, they can offer a very high form of service. They can indeed love their neighbours as themselves, and they will recognize and appreciate that the religious motive is necessary for the conduct of life, if it is to be as fine as possible.

From the Synagogue indeed can be evolved a high standard of life which challenges the loyalty of every member, and if you cannot find the standard you think right to accept, if you cannot discover in the services the stimulus you need, I would ask you whether you seek to offer something better which can be assimilated into Synagogue life, and if you don't, whether you are not seriously at fault? We must not increase the religious apathy and indifference when we believe we can benefit mankind spiritually. Are you shocked at this claim? Do you think we are arrogant in making it? Are you aggrieved because people of other faiths lead equally good or better lives, and must also have a claim to influence humanity in its spiritual growth. I believe in the Light of the Perfect Day, but I believe we can only reach it if each group trims its own wick, and is loyal and enthusiastic, understanding and loving. Just consider some of the things we Jews have already done. We have given the Bible to the world. The world has taken our Bible, but not away from us. They have asked to share it, and we the people of the book are not always alive to the value of our possessions. Does the

Bible have an important place in the personal life, and in your home life? Unless we discipline our lives under the teaching of the Bible, it is possible that we shall not be able to convince the world for all time of its value. Our Bible gives us a fine code of morality, and tells us that a good Jew must live in accordance with its highest teaching. Do you find time to read or to study the Bible? A great deal can be done if you are prepared to set aside every day a few minutes for this all important work. We have told the world that religion is based on morality. We must give practical object lessons, and not only the book in which the fact is proclaimed. We have given the world the Sabbath principle, a day on which we rest and rejoice, pray, think and study. Do you use at least part of your Sabbath in that way? We have shown the world the supreme importance of social justice which establishes the right of every man to live and work in decency and to fulfil himself in peace. Are we always sufficiently aware as employers of labour, or as responsible citizens, that we do not sin against our own ideal? We have affirmed the sanctity of home life. Do we remember to consecrate it by family services, by chastity, by holy joy? We exalt the idea that the whole of man is holy to the Lord. Do we do all we can to develop physically, intellectually and spiritually? We appreciate the beauty of life. Do we do reverence to the beauty of nature as the creation of God; are we always careful not to prostitute art to gratify unworthy desires? We have affirmed the value of truth in the inwards parts of every man and woman, and in his relations to his neighbours. Do we always refrain from giving false witness, or from backbiting acquaintances in order to gain a certain degree of popularity for ourselves? We have given the world the conception of the One God who is Eternal, and who has created man in His image. Do we always express the Fatherhood of God in our devotion to the brotherhood of man, to peace and democracy and the removal of all obstructions to the healthy development of mankind? God has put eternity in our hearts and so has given us for ever in which to realize ourselves, and to cling to our beloved. Do we actually believe in an infinite future which overcomes death towards which we can go with invincible hope and faith, believing that since God is rightousness, truth and beauty and love, these realities must prevail?[10]

A SUNDAY SABBATH?

How we are to observe the Sabbath is a question which each one must settle for himself. The details cannot be considered here. But, broadly speaking, two things are desirable: the first is that there should be a day of rest; the second is that we should spend, wherever possible, one or two hours of it in the public worship of God. Now the present conditions of life sometimes prevent both the one and the other. The Christian day of rest being Sunday, a large number of Jews, and a considerable number of Jewesses, are more or less bound to 'work' upon Saturdays. One of the most important questions, which liberal Judaism has to consider is, what attitude it should take up towards this urgent and complicated problem.

It would not be irrational to advocate a transference of the Sabbath from Saturday to Sunday. There is no divine virtue in one particular day. The old orthodox view was that God created the world in six days and rested on the seventh, and it was undoubtedly believed that if the Saturdays were followed back far enough, you would ultimately come to the very Sabbath upon which God rested. 'Time' began on Sunday. If this were so, and if we still believe that God Himself directly ordered us to observe the Sabbath (that is, the seventh day, the Saturday), and to rest upon it, it would be monstrous to suggest any change or transference. Such suggestion would amount to blasphemy. But for 'liberal' Jews this supernatural sanction for the Sabbath has passed away. Thus, if the whole of European and American Jewry could transfer the Sabbath from Saturday and Sunday, and if all Jews were faithfully to observe the Sunday by rest and prayer and worship, and if they did not lose their Jewish consciousness by the transference, but, on the contrary, deepened and vivified it, then the change, so far from being a loss, might be a benefit.

It is, however, exceedingly doubtful whether these provisos could be carried into effect. It is commonly alleged that where a 'Sunday Sabbath' has been attempted, the speedy result is that neither Saturday nor Sunday is properly observed. In other words, average human nature (I will not say average Jewish human nature) has not the self-sacrifice, the strength of mind and tenacity of purpose sufficient to make the change of religious effectiveness and value. For it is a question of will power.

It would need strong resolution and fixed determination for any Jew to transfer to Sunday the feelings which his early training and the lives of his ancestors have centred upon Saturday. Yet by sufficient doggedness and sacrifice, and above all by the most patient care devoted to the education of children, there seems no absolute or overwhelming reason why a new generation could not arise who would observe Sunday with a full and eager Jewish consciousness, and in all religious solemnity and fruitfulness.

Meanwhile for the present – and this book is written to meet present needs – there is no question of transference of the Sabbath from Saturday to Sunday. We have to consider things as they are, and to make the best of them.

First of all, let us regard the Sabbath as a day of rest and change. We are not merely to cease from work, but we are also to make it a different day from other days. It is emphatically to be a day of 'delight', but it is also to be a 'holy day', 'the holy of the Lord'. It is to be a day of peace, of repose, of 'collection', of refreshment. The pleasures of the Sabbath must be other than the pleasures of work days – less noisy and less mundane, more intimate, retired and inward.

Now, many Jews and Jewesses are unable to give up their work upon the Sabbath. A large percentage of the 'working classes' are habitually compelled to violate the Sabbath. This fact is the one great argument for the transference of the day from Saturday to Sunday. I cannot enter here upon the economic and social side of the question in this place. Suffice it to say that both for the 'poor' and the 'well-to-do,' – for the 'lower', the 'middle' and the 'upper classes' alike – it is hard to see how a certain amount of Saturday labour can be avoided. For my present purpose I have the more 'well-to-do' sections of the community in mind. It would be impossible to argue that parents should only send their sons and daughters into occupations and professions where the Sabbath can be observed. We are Englishmen, and we must accept the responsibilities and difficulties of complete emancipation. To say, for instance, that no Jew ought to become a barrister or a civil servant would be an untenable proposition, and yet, at the present time, these professions almost infallibly involve labour upon some portions of the Sabbath day. In very many branches of business and commerce it is, I believe, hopeless to achieve success if no work is to be done upon Saturdays.

The conflict must, therefore, for the present be left as it stands. If the Saturday be maintained, the Sabbath must be violated; to the day on which it would not be violated it cannot be transferred. I am far from saying that for many and many a year to come the second statement will not be as true as the first. Only let none of us shut our eyes. We do not improve facts by refusing to look at them. We do not annul them by declining to believe in their existence. On the contrary, the facts must be faced and borne in mind. Only so can their evil effects be palliated, and their solution ultimately be achieved.

If, however, the Sabbath must be violated by many Jews for reasons which none of us can deny or demolish, so much the more urgent is it that those who *can* observe it should observe it, and that those who *have* to violate it should limit their violation to the smallest possible number of hours. Above all, there should be no voluntary desecration and misuse for the purpose of *mere* convenience and *unsuitable* enjoyment.[11]

LIBERAL JUDAISM AND CHRISTIANITY

We today want to know ... are there Jewish equivalents for certain Christian conceptions? Do, or should, any of these conceptions form part of our modern Jewish religion, and if so, how have we obtained them, or how should we mould them? Have these Christian conceptions Jewish origins or parallels, or were these dropped out of the Jewish consciousness or the Jewish religion when the more deliberate opposition to Christianity began to grow up? A certain Christian conception may be in the forefront of the Christian religion and of Christian theology: in its specific Christian form it may be inconsistent with Judaism, whether orthodox or liberal; nevertheless, it may have distinct Jewish parallels in old Jewish thought or in old Jewish literature. But because the conception became predominantly Christian, and a characteristic of Christianity, did it drop out, or was it deliberately excluded, from Jewish religion and Jewish theology. What was the result? This must be considered and decided in each particular case. It may be that Judaism was rendered in some given point one-sided. The conception in question may have provided a certain balance. The lack of it may have tended to exaggeration, aridity, one-sidedness. Again, it may even be that a certain Christian conception may supply a corrective to a particular Jewish inadequacy, or a supplement to a particular Jewish doctrine. The conception, being cast in Christian form, was repellent to Jewish thinkers, and the result may have been that Judaism was rendered still more one-sided. For if a certain religion X lacks a certain conception Y, the omission may not for X be of any great consequence, or again, it may easily be supplied. But if a rival religion, Z, adopts this conception, and gives it a place of prominence in its own system, what may happen? The religion X may now make a dead set against Y; it may declare Y to be false, dangerous and antithetical opposed to itself. Instead of finding out the truth about Y, X may set itself to caricature and condemn Y, with the result that X becomes consciously one-sided, which is far more serious than being unconsciously one-sided ...

It may be of importance to find out what, if any, are the Christian conceptions which have no old Jewish parallels, but which, nevertheless, are not essentially opposed to Judaism, but which on the contrary, in a modified form, could be adopted with profit and consistency. Such additions might merely add volume and depth to Judaism, and correct any existing one-sidedness, exaggeration, or roughness of edge. There seems to me little doubt that Judaism has suffered from Christianity in a very different way from what has usually been supposed! It has suffered in keeping half an eye on it. In some respects, Judaism would have developed more freely and naturally, if it had never known that there was such a religion as Christianity existing in the world. It would have mattered less if Christianity had been a tiny religion in an out-of-the-way portion of the globe. But Christianity became a universal religion: the religion of Europe and of Western civilization; partly the creator of that civilisation. It partly absorbed, and was itself partly modified by, the best thought of Greece and Rome. Hence, the rejection by Judaism, of all Christian conceptions may have meant that it rejected a great body of thought which was not merely and purely Christian. It may have rejected much that was, or could be made, supplementary and complementary to itself. By too wholesale rejection it may have rejected what was true as well as what was false, and it may have narrowed its own outlook and its own doctrines more than was needful or desirable. And it may have done all this in modern times more than in ancient times; it may even be doing this today. It may be that Talmudic Judaism is more full of living, varied, sometimes, I admit, inconsistent ideas than is the Judaism of our modern textbooks or sermons. Instead of being more one-sided than they are, it may be in some ways less one-sided, more alive, more responsive to, more expressive of, various aspects of truth, various sides of experience.[12]

LIBERAL JEWS AND THE NEW TESTAMENT

Even though we hold that Jesus erroneously supposed himself to be the Messiah predicted by the prophets, it does not follow that he was not a great religious and ethical teacher. Isaiah was wrong in several of his predictions, but he is a great teacher all the same. Jesus may have been wrong as to his Messiahship, but none the less he may have been a great teacher. Doubtless the picture of him drawn in the Gospels is sometimes idealized and inaccurate, but none the less may the teachings attributed to him be of profound religious value, and contain many 'supplementary and complementary truths.' It is simply not the case that one cannot separate the teaching of Jesus about religion and morality from the claim, only rarely ascribed to him, of thrusting himself between man and God as a necessary intermediary and introducer. To the doctrine contained in Matthew 11:25–30[13] liberal Jews will be as opposed as their orthodox brethren. Jews had found rest in God before Jesus came, and without his help we have found rest in God ever since. Our history proves it. Otherwise we could not show more martyrs than all the sects of Christianity put together. But even if Jesus said the words contained in those six verses, which is extremely doubtful, that does not make *other* words ascribed to him less worthy of our adoption and our praise.

It is this sifting and critical manner of regarding the Gospels and the New Testament which must also be applied to the third difficulty, the alleged higher doctrine on the one hand and its enfeeblement of pure monotheism upon the other. The old oppositions are seen to be erroneous and exaggerated. There may be some new things in the book which are bad, and some new things which are good. The notion that the Old Testament teaches a God of justice, the New Testament a God of love, that the keynote of the one book is retribution, of the other book pity, is childish and absurd. We shall rather say that in some respects some passages of the New Testament show a declension from the *highest* conceptions of the Old Testament, while in other matters there are passages in the New Testament which supplement and complete the doctrines of the Old Testament. I would venture to say provisionally that our conceptions of character and of sin, of our duty to the sinner and the outcast, and of religious inwardness and spiritual intensity, can be heightened and deepened by a study of the New Testament.

Nobody should be more qualified for a calm and impartial investigation of this book than liberal Jews. We need have no difficulty in accepting from it whatever is good and true. We need not be excited about it, whether to refute or advocate. What is good and true in it is divine, because what is good and true is of God. Liberal Judaism does not teach that all goodness and truth in religion are or can be contained in one book; its equilibrium and fundamental tenets are not upset if the Jews who composed the New Testament, amid much error, said also several things that were new and true. The Jews who wrote the Talmud did the same ...

But all this does not commit us to any particular view of the central hero. Jesus, so far as we can gather, was a great and inspired teacher but what he precisely thought and taught will always remain obscure. The Gospels were written by the disciples of his disciples for purposes of edification. They idealise on the one hand; they darken on the other. To increase the lonely greatness of the hero, the disciples must be made stupid, the people ungrateful, hardhearted, wicked. To estimate the Jewish religion (as Christian theologians do) from the New Testament is to produce a caricature; to find a portrait of Jesus in the Gospels is to look for a photograph in an idealised picture, painted several years after the subject's death.

Nor can the New Testament be acknowledged by Jews as a part of their own Bible. The Hebrew Scriptures remains by itself; it is the charter of Judaism. The New Testament is, after all, the charter of another creed. So things must remain for many a year. To read a chapter of the New Testament in a 'liberal' synagogue would provoke misunderstanding, even though a piece of a modern religious poem, such as *In Memoriam*, which could not have been written outside of the New Testament, does not. But, outside the synagogue, it is right for liberal Jews to read the New Testament; it is their duty, and it is within their power, to appraise and estimate it correctly without prejudice or passion. What on these lines we appropriate and admire can never make us less devoted to Judaism, because what we admire and what we appropriate will itself be Jewish, the 'supplement and complement' and the expression of Jewish doctrine and of Jewish truth.[14]

WHY JEWS DO NOT BELIEVE IN CHRIST

'To believe in Jesus Christ' originally meant to believe that he was the Messiah whom the Jews in the time of Jesus hoped for and expected. Orthodox Jews, who still believe in the coming of the Messiah, deny that Jesus was the Messiah because he did not fulfil the role of the Messiah, which was to restore Israel and to inaugurate the consummation of human history in the Kingdom of God. For Liberal Jews the question whether Jesus was the Messiah does not arise, they do not hold the belief in a personal Messiah, though their interpretation of Judaism includes the hope for a Messianic age.

But the epithet 'Christ' came to mean in Christian belief much more than 'the Messiah'. In Christianity Jesus is the Redeemer and Saviour. For Judaism, God, and God alone, is the Redeemer and Saviour of mankind and of men. But, Christianity would answer, Jesus was God. That is what it means 'to believe in Christ,' to believe in the doctrine of the Incarnation. That doctrine is not interpreted alike by all Christians. But, however it is interpreted, it means that Jesus was not just a man, or just a great man; it means that he was different from all other men who have lived, or will live, in being more than a man; that he was a divine man, a man who was all God.

Now, Judaism teaches that human beings have a divine quality; they have, to put it simply, something of God in them. The idea originated in such verses in the Jewish Bible as 'man was created in the image of God' and 'ye are the children of God'. But Judaism has a conception of God which precludes the belief that any man could, so to speak, have the whole of God in him. For God is the God of the universe, and no part of the universe can contain Him. More than that, the whole universe cannot contain Him. He is more than the universe. 'The heaven of heavens cannot contain thee', says the Bible. And there is a Rabbinic saying: 'The universe is not the place of God, but God is the place of the universe', which may be interpreted that the universe does not contain God, but God contains the universe. Moreover, Judaism has always emphasized that there is a difference in essence between God and man. Though they are related, no one can be both God and man: they are essentially different. That is the chief and fundamental reason why Jews do not 'believe in Christ'. There are subsidiary reasons. One is that the stories told about him, which are in the Gospels, do not give any ground for such a belief. But the main reason is that to 'believe in Christ' is contrary to the Jewish belief in God.

Other beliefs followed from the belief in the Incarnation. Whereas Judaism taught that God is one, indivisible, but manifesting Himself in an infinite number of ways, Christianity taught, and teaches, that though God is one, yet He is a trinity, manifesting himself in the three ways described in the formula: Father, Son and Holy Ghost (*i.e.* holy spirit). I cannot attempt to explain the doctrine of the trinity, for I cannot claim to understand it fully; but it is evident that there is a vast difference between the Christian belief in the trinity of God and the Jewish belief in His unity.

Again, the place given to Jesus in the Christian scheme of salvation distinguishes it from Judaism. It is the central teaching of Christianity that Jesus is the Saviour for every individual and the Saviour for all humanity, that through his life, his crucifixion, and his present influence, the world will be saved, and every individual man can be saved by believing in him. In this sense, Jesus stands between God and man, as a go-between, a mediator. The Jew does not believe that about Jesus, nor about any man. Judaism teaches that there is a direct and immediate relation between God and every individual human being. Everyone, no matter how unworthy he feels, and we are all unworthy, can, with his prayers, trusting to God's love, come to Him to ask for forgiveness for sin, and for help in his endeavours towards goodness.

Similarly, while Christianity teaches that salvation must come through Jesus, that he will save humanity from all that is evil, that through him, or because of him, God will save humanity,

Judaism teaches that God Himself will save humanity directly because He is good and all-loving, and he lays on every man the duty to make himself an instrument for God's saving power.

There can be, and there is, I believe, no objection from the Jewish point of view to the view that Jesus was a great teacher. So were Confucius, Buddha or Mohammed. Jews must, however, have a greater interest in Jesus than in any of them because he was a Jew. He was born a Jew and he died a Jew. If he criticized some of the religious practices of his time, so did the Prophets before him; and like the Prophets, he was loyal to the Jewish religion and attached to the Jewish people. But any conception of Jesus and his work beyond that of a great religious teacher is outside Judaism.

There are, however, some Christians who do not believe in the Trinity or the Incarnation, so that their conception of God appears to be like that of Judaism, and their religious ideas generally appear to be like those held by Liberal Jews. They differ, however, from Liberal Jews in several ways. They hold the Christian conception of the relation between God and man, while Liberal Judaism naturally holds the Jewish conception. Moreover, Jesus is for Christians who do not believe in the Incarnation still more than a great man, one who was not only greater than all other great men but one who was in essence different from all human beings, that he was unique. However much Jews may admire the personality and teachings of Jesus given in the Gospels, he remains for them a man.

There is a further difference between Liberal Judaism and Liberal Christianity in that they have different traditions. Liberal Judaism is based on Jewish tradition, Liberal Christianity follows Christian tradition. The spirit of the Jewish tradition differs from that of the Christian tradition. The different traditions give them different religious backgrounds and different guides to thought and conduct. Moreover, the difference in the histories and essential beliefs of the two religions begets a difference between their attitudes towards life. It cannot be defined sharply; it is largely a difference in emphasis. Both religions, for example, attach value to man's life on earth, and both look on it as a preparation for another life. The Christian tradition has perhaps emphasized the second part more than the Jewish tradition did, and the Jewish tradition emphasized the first more. The difference in emphasis issues from somewhat divergent valuations of this world. Liberal Jew and Liberal Christian agree in some beliefs – just as Orthodox Jews and Orthodox Christians agree in some beliefs – but there are also important differences between them. If, however, some Christians hold beliefs like those of Liberal Judaism, they do not make our position less Jewish, but their position more nearly Jewish; and as Jews we should be deeply grateful that others are coming to the Jewish conception of God and His relation to the universe ...[15]

GEORGE ELIOT AND SOLOMON MAIMON

That George Eliot was well acquainted with certain aspects of Jewish history is fairly clear from her writings. But there is collateral evidence of an interesting kind that proves the same fact quite conclusively, I think.

It will be remembered that Daniel Deronda went into a second-hand book-shop and bought a small volume for half a crown, thereby making the acquaintance of Ezra Cohen. Some time back I had in my hands the identical book that George Eliot purchased which formed the basis of the incident. The book may now be seen in Dr Wilhams's Library, Gordon Square, London. The few words in which George Eliot dismisses the book in her novel would hardly lead one to gather how carefully and conscientiously she had read the volume, which has since been translated into English by Dr J. Clark Murray. She, of course, bought and read the original German.

The book is Solomon Maimon's Autobiography, a fascinating piece of self-revelation and of history ... Maimon, cynic and sceptic, was a man all head and no heart, but he was not without 'character', in one sense of the word. He forms a necessary link in the progress of modern Jews towards their newer culture. Schiller and Goethe admired him considerably, and, as we shall soon see, George Eliot was a careful student of his celebrated pages. Any reader who takes the book up will hardly lay it down until he has finished the first part, at least.

Several marginal and other notes in the copy of the Autobiography that belonged to George Eliot are, I am convinced, in her own handwriting, and I propose to print here some of her jottings, all of which are in pencil, but carefully written. Above the Introduction, she writes: 'This book might mislead many readers not acquainted with other parts of Jewish history.

But for a worthy account (in brief) of Judaism and Rabbinism, see p. 150.' This reference takes one to the fifteenth chapter of the Autobiography. Indeed, George Eliot was right as to the misleading tendency of a good deal in Maimon's 'wonderful piece of autobiography', as she terms the work in 'Daniel Deronda'. She returns to the attack on p. 36 of her copy, where she has jotted, 'See infra, p. 150 *et seq.* for a better-informed view of Talmudic study.'

How carefully George Eliot read! The pagination of 207 is printed wrongly as 160; she corrects it! She corrects *Kimesi* into *Kimchi* on p. 48, *Rabasse* into 'R. Ashe' on p. 163. On p. 59 she writes, 'According to the Talmud no one is eternally damned.' Perhaps her statement needs some slight qualification. Again (p. 62), 'Rashi, i.e. Rabbi Shelomoh ben Isaak, whom Buxtorf mistakenly called Jarchi.' It was really to Raymund Martini that this error goes back. But George Eliot could not know it. On p. 140, Maimon begins, 'Accordingly, I sought to explain all this in the following way', to which George Eliot appends the note, 'But this is simply what the Cabbala teaches – not his own ingenious explanation.'

It is interesting to find George Eliot occasionally defending Judaism against Maimon. On p. 16 he talks of the 'abuse of Rabbinism', in that the Rabbis tacked on new laws to old texts. 'Its origin', says George Eliot's pencilled jotting, 'was the need for freedom to modify laws' – a fine remark. On p. 173, where Maimon again talks of the Rabbinical method of evolving all sorts of moral truths by the oddest exegesis, she writes, 'The method has been constantly pursued in various forms by Christian Teachers.' On p. 186 Maimon makes merry at the annulment of vows previous to the Day of Atonement. George Eliot writes, 'These are religious vows – not engagements between man and man.' ...

It is a pleasure, indeed, to find a fresh confirmation that George Eliot's favourable impression of Judaism was based on a very adequate acquaintance with its history.[16]

A CALL FOR LIBERAL JEWISH THEOLOGIANS

We need philosophic theologians who shall neither be afraid of Christian doctrine on the one hand, nor be on the constant search for contrasts on the other. Problems connected with transcendence and immanence, with omnipotence and creation, with the relation of God to suffering and evil, still need much examination; Jewish teaching on these subjects needs development and expansion. So, too, as to the divine character; as to wrath and love, righteousness and love, holiness and love; here, too, there is much work to be done, and much room for theologians and philosophers, who will not wish to impoverish Judaism by insisting on differences and contrasts, but will rather seek to enrich it by finding out what the great minds of other religions have thought and taught, and how much is consistent with Judaism, and valuable and worthy of adoption and incorporation, and how much must be rejected; how much can be translated into Jewish terminology (for, after all, what a large amount is a question of terminology!), and how much is untranslatable, undesirable, and untrue. We need theologians who do not want to sit in corners and erect peculiar systems of their own, but who are willing to profit and learn even from those whose traditions and accents are other than their own. We have done a good deal but much remains to do.

Besides other points we have to re-examine and set forth afresh the doctrine of the divine unity. It will be needful for Liberal Jewish theologians to consider the new modern interpretations of the doctrine of the Trinity, and to discuss how far these are, and how far they are not, in accordance with Jewish views of the unity. It might, for example, seem as if there were little in Dean Rashdall's interpretation of the Trinity which a Jew could not accept. But it will have to be pointed out how the Dean appears to allow that many forms of popular Trinitarianism at any rate have been somewhat tainted with Tritheism, and that the new teaching seems to us nearer to Judaism than to many manifestations of Christianity. What I am concerned about is that Jewish theologians shall make it clear that the Jewish doctrine of the unity does not tend to impoverish the divine nature, but only to emphasize its complete harmony and self-consistency. God may have as many aspects as you please so long as there is no opposition between the one and the other, so long as the pure unity of the one self-consciousness is rigidly maintained.[17]

THE ROLE OF WOMEN IN RELIGIOUS LIFE

Today women are conscious that their sons and daughters are slipping away from institutional religion. They are less concerned than men about loyalty to tradition. Their great desire is to attract their children to the Synagogue by making the services understood and alive. Judaism is based on reason and emotion. Women being more emotional than men must help in rendering that element strong and pure. Liberal Judaism is criticized by those who do not enter deeply into our fellowship because it is said to be cold. Women must increase the warmth of life. In our women's societies women are so often satisfied to contribute to the upkeep of the religion school without desiring as adults to improve their own education and to clarify their own understanding of the history, principles and practices of Judaism. They provide beautifully for the social events of the Synagogue, but are unconcerned in improving the aesthetic influence of public worship and bringing their own experiences in depth and sincerity to the united prayers of their fellow congregants. Yet they care so much for beauty; they are so easily moved by contact with the divine; in their own lives they have found the connection between morality and religion and the power of prayer, which should make this union a reality. The time has surely come when they must extend and increase their influence in Synagogue life.

It is the women who today can do much to arrest the deterioration of home life. A rottenness has set in which threatens the very foundation of those sanctities which have an essentially Jewish value. The social conscience is apparently little disturbed today by infidelity between husband and wife. A careless shrug or a flippant word is often all the interest shown in the fact that a home has been broken up. The position of the children of broken marriages is, it is agreed, unfortunate and often painful, but the best must be made of it. The moral code has fallen from its exalted place. Not only is the relation between men and women deteriorating generally, but there is also a looseness with regard to loyalty in word and deed. Women who understand the disastrous results of this decadence must examine their own faith and seek to strengthen it. They must then seek with all the power at their command to prove that Judaism is not a verbal creed. As our ancestors taught us, it inspires a righteous way of life and depends for its existence on our effort after righteousness and truth. After all Liberal Jews are not expected to receive their religion from the past and to remember its importance when it is convenient for them to do so. They must not use the observances their ancestors used when these are pleasing to them and cast others away without examination. These observances must only be discarded if they have no ethical or religious value, if perhaps they have been shown by scholars to be based on myth or superstition. It is not enough to disregard observance because it entails sacrifice or because it is considered by the members of one's social set or even by members of one's family as out of date or old fashioned. Sacrifice helps to purify the soul; independent thinking is essential to the men or women who wish to serve their God. Moreover, each generation is meant to add a contribution to the truth which their predecessors have discovered, and women as well as men have to respond to this challenge, to this trust.

I have tried to put forward my view that women's contribution to religion is in the field of religious education, in the creation of permanent peace, and in the quickening of the moral sense in her own life and in the lives of those whom she can influence. I have emphasized some of the positive ways in which she is called upon to fulfil her obligations. There is also a negative aspect to these important considerations.

Women can increase or degrade the influence of the religion school. It is not enough for them to join women's societies in providing splendid equipment for the school and the library. Every woman must also know what the child is taught and refrain even at the time of examinations from placing the requirements of the so-called secular school first, or in disparaging the religion school teachers by contrasting their skill with those of the secular school teachers. A mother must not weaken the background of the religion school by lightly saying: 'We don't do that any more. I have no interest in the subject. I have forgotten all my Hebrew and am all right without it, as I never go to the Synagogue,' when the child comes home full of enthusiasm about the lesson he has had and the meaning of the home observances, so interesting and colourful, which he never sees in his own home ...

Our women must also gain knowledge and use it in the best

possible way. They must use their gifts of heart as well as of mind; they must show how to express religion in life; they must prove that these two are coextensive. Judaism must be studied and understood before it can be lived. It can only be lived when it is loved. Women in the Reform Movement have happily come down from the Synagogue galleries and entered into the Congregational lives of their Synagogues. They must show how their thought and actions are purified and illuminated by faith. They must raise the standard of citizenship for their own children and then for the general community by preparing their young people to face civic and industrial problems. If there is corruption in a city, mothers must help directly and indirectly in banishing it. If a girl or boy questions why no interest is taken in a civic election, it is no reply to say 'I can't take an interest, the corruption is as iniquitous.' You use the cities' supply of light and heat. Women have to create purity, wisdom and zeal in all kinds of social reform. As Mazzini the great Italian patriot said: To sanctify the Family more and more and to bring it ever closer to the country; this is your mission. Sanctify the Family in the unity of love. Make it a temple in which you may sacrifice together to the country. I do not know if you will be happy, but I do know that if you do this there will come to you even in the midst of adversity a sense of serene peace, the repose of a tranquil conscience, which will give you strength in every trial and will keep an azure space open before your eyes in every tempest.

In the days of our grandparents women were expected to keep a Jewish home by observing all the dietary laws. Even today a potential proselyte told me she thought she had a good knowledge of Judaism as she lived next door to a kosher butcher. That was the religious stimulus given to her by the parents of her fiancé.

A woman may also light the candles on the Sabbath Eve. But may I tell my readers that they must do infinitely more. Their candles must stand as symbols of truth and purity and love. These great divine attributes must be given to the nation to which they belong, and because they believe in the rule of God, they must know that He expects from them the most zealous cooperation in achieving this great purpose, for so they will be helping in their small imperfect way to build God's Kingdom.[18]

WORKING GIRLS

No study of boy life can be complete without some reference
to the 'girl in the background'; her influence has been recognized since the day when Adam attempted to justify himself
in the Garden of Eden. Indeed, we believe that the power of
women over men is based on a law of nature against which
rebellion is impossible. It is one of the cherished principles
underlying the national life of countries, which boast of Western
civilization that the influence of the 'girl in the background'
tends towards purity, temperance, righteousness, and peace.

> O woman, lovely woman! Nature made thee
> To temper man; we had been brutes without you:
> Angels are painted fair to look like you;
> There's in you all that we believe of heaven;
> Amazing brightness, purity, and truth,
> Eternal joy and everlasting love.

This faith was embodied in the forms of chivalry, which, in spite
of their narrow artificiality, inflamed the popular imagination
during the Middle Ages. Gradually the influence of this same
faith broadened, until to day it serves as the sanctification of
home life and the life of the State. The fact that woman has
inspired most of the evil as well as most of the good known to
human experience has happily not shaken our belief in her
blessed potentialities.

In this chapter it is our purpose to discuss the relations
between working girls and working boys. But we must at the
outset of our inquiry recognize that there is one factor in these
relations, which baffles any attempt at scientific investigation.
Womanly charm, the *ewig weibliche*, existing apparently by spontaneous generation, appears again and again to beautify and
ennoble the lives of our working girls. Under present conditions, however, the training and environment of these girls
militates against the existence and growth of the *best* in woman-
hood. The limits of space render it impossible to make a comparative study of the conditions prevailing in other classes of
society. Otherwise we should probably be obliged to admit that
even among the most cultured, the relations of girls to boys has
not yet reached its highest development. It is only in modern

times that conscious effort has been made to teach girls that they do not exist as the mere supplements to men, but that they possess the dignity of human beings with, infinite possibilities and definite responsibilities. Heretofore they were as far as possible protected from contact with ugliness and evil. Today they are being equipped with that moral, physical, and intellectual strength by which the world's pain may be combated.

We want to see in girls the finest perceptions of truth, beauty, and purity, the greatest capacity for self-restraint and for the highest joys of self-sacrifice. While freely and gratefully admitting that these qualities *are* to be found not infrequently among working girls whose lives have not been subjected to much refining influence from without, we believe that social effort can be directed to rendering these instances of feminine nobility less miraculous in character. It is education, physical, mental, and religious education that must ultimately be the chief factor in influencing the lives of working girls in their relation to boys ...

In the economic world the girl's place is inferior to that of the boy. She is of less value, for she is less well trained. She knows herself to be a fairly cheap article, and this fact lessens her sense of personal responsibility. Boys and girls very seldom compete in trade; they may perform different processes in the same industry, but their work is almost invariably quite distinct, and the boys' work is generally more skilled. The girl is glad to enter those trades in which she can pick up a few shillings quickly, for her wage-earning faculties improve her position in the matrimonial market. Indeed, her industrial life is only of temporary interest to the working girl, who regards it merely as a preliminary to marriage. Therefore she is disinclined to spend much time in training, and prefers unskilled work in which wage-earning begins immediately.

The absence of industrial organization among girls further tends to diminish their sense of personal responsibility. There is little incentive to good work beyond the desirability of good pay. The working girl does not realize that she can contribute to the honour of her trade. She merely knows that if she does not do well enough to satisfy the requirements of her employer, a hundred other girls will be ready to take her place in the factory. As soon as the factory working hours are over her responsibilities are at an end, and she is ready to forget, as far as her weariness will permit, the drudgery of the day in the enjoyment of any fun which may come within her reach. It is only when we realize the monotony of the workshop life that we can understand why the craving for excitement is almost a necessary element in the working girl's composition. As a child she was dependent on street incidents for most of her pleasures. She is not as an adult impervious to the nervous excitement which characterizes all sections of the community at the present day, and this craving is, of course, intensified by her limited experience of other forms of happiness, and by the dullness and repression of her working life. Her very nature cries out for change and amusement. She loves crudities, for she has not been initiated into refined joys. The susceptibility and sensitiveness of girl nature are the sources of its highest potentialities. But these very qualities render girls more liable than boys to surrender their best selves to the degrading influences of their environment. It is because of their individualistic, irresponsible, and pleasure – loving tendencies that we find so many unsatisfactory elements in the working girl's influence over the boy. Flirting is the main object of their intercourse. Public opinion demands apparently little else. Anyone travelling on the Great Eastern Railway in a third-class carriage on a Sunday can never have gathered from the prevailing conversation any suggestion of serious comradeship. It is the talk of children, but it is not child talk. We ask in fear, what does it promise for the future? Flirtation affords amusement, and even when it passes the boundary of pure fun, and becomes degrading in character, the elders listen and are not offended. They know from personal experience the monotony of workshop life, and they would be loath to interfere with Sunday play. The boys and girls see no serious meaning in love-making; they are playing a game. They have been trained less to reverence one another than to protect their own independence.[19]

WOMEN RABBIS

Men seem to me to prosper intellectually most successfully when they can fully indulge in investigation and scientific reasoning; women do so in imagination and in the full use of the creative spirit. It is said that a man climbs slowly step by step up the mountain of knowledge only to find sitting at the top a woman who cannot explain how she got there.

We are a people of eastern origin and it has taken us a very long time to arrive at the conclusion that men and women have an equal right to free development and unrestricted powers of service. Through the revelation of God which led us to accept His truths, Jewish women in history advanced more quickly than their contemporaries in acquiring human rights. They have not yet reached the stage when equal rights should be allowed them if they desire to acquire them in all professions.

As a matter of convention, the majority of Jews would not favour women in the Rabbinate, although in other departments in western countries and in India they are allowed without restriction to attain the highest professional dignity. As doctors, lawyers, politicians and actors, they are not debarred through sex of the highest positions. But the eastern idea of physical inferiority still interferes with their position in the Ministry.

One of the objects of the Jewish Liberals in England when they founded their movement at the beginning of this century was to establish the equality of men and women. Their rights to take part in the government of the Synagogue was not accepted in the Orthodox section of the community. In the Liberal division they were fully accepted and their position has influenced the general community which now, in some part at least, allows women as seatholders and as members of Councils. But we owe it to our great leader, Rabbi Dr Mattuck that the principle of allowing equal status to men and women as Lay Ministers was accorded. There was unfortunately no woman qualified by scholarship and ministerial training to enter the Rabbinate, but a woman Lay Minister was inducted and given the leadership of a Congregation.[20] We are hoping that others will be trained for the full Rabbinate when Liberal Theological colleges are established.

From the practical point of view, we have to admit that today few Congregations would accept the spiritual leadership of a woman if a man were available. So candidates dependent on this work for their living would have to hesitate before accepting the training even when freely offered to them. But prejudice is removed by time. There is little doubt that if women are prepared to recognize that their Ministry must depend on the development of their full intellectual powers, as well as those of heart and spirit, they will before long see their services eagerly accepted by Congregations. If they have a feeling of vocation, their God will help them to develop and use that feeling to the full. They must prove their worth. They must exalt themselves through service, and never rely on any minor personal attraction to render them acceptable for Synagogue leadership. A Minister must share the joys and aspirations, sorrows and frustrations of the whole of humanity. There must be no artificial limitation to their human interests and sympathies. They must learn humbly and reverently to understand some small part of God's revelation of truth and then be prepared to give of their highest thought and feeling to a Congregation who would desire their services. Through service to God, they will find the way to serve a Congregation of men, women and children. If they can do this, they will surely be invited before long to join the Jewish Rabbinate. Why not?[21]

WORKING GIRLS' CLUBS

In the club, the leaders have to direct their girls' energy to the realization of the highest standards of happiness, the happiness of self-development and the happiness of service. By dint of technical art-teaching a girl is initiated into the joys of creation. The production of a beautiful piece of handiwork stimulates her self-respect. Her corporate feeling is roused when she joins a choral class, or a class for physical drill, and contributes her individual energy to the general success. Factory life makes little claim on the individual capacity of the worker; she therefore finds recreation in simple brainwork, which does not overtax her physical strength. The passing of standards does not inspire the average pupil with any great reverence for knowledge. The effort to study subjects which she had always thought easy, but which in reality call for long and patient perseverance, tends to correct in adolescence the false impressions conveyed by a short school-life. The girl's outlook on life is readjusted by the club – she realizes the power of truth and purity, and is training to seek these essentials even in her intercourse with friends.

The club member's sense of responsibility is further stimulated by her desire to uphold the honour of her club. Gradually she herself is required to take a share in its management. She

sees how her own conduct affects those with whom she is
brought in contact, and her training in citizenship begins as
soon as she is subjected to the discipline of associated interests.
When she is away from the club this training helps her to
triumph over the temptations and difficulties of her life.

Through friendship with women of culture, working girls
become acquainted with the pleasures of peace afforded by
reading, by country life, by the contemplation of works of art.
Their dangerous craving for excitement is counteracted by
indulgence in healthy recreation. They are no longer so inclined
to accept flirtation as their only possible escape from the monotony of their lives. They have other interests besides the supreme
one of courtship. If in the factory they feel of small account,
they have in the club to set a truer value on themselves. New
possibilities are revealed to them, and their lives become irradi-
ated by ideals. Men are not slow to recognize self-control in
girls; and the best results of club life are to be seen in the
increased respect with which the members are treated by their
boy friends. Perhaps the harvest of results would be greater if
club-leaders would themselves more generally recognize their
responsibilities. Like other philanthropists, club-workers are too
easily satisfied with fringing the problems with which they
should endeavour to grapple. They peep down the abyss in
which the underfed, the ill-housed, and badly clothed work out
their life's drama, and then they turn their energies to surface
polishing. They try to make their girls conduct themselves well
in the clubs, and interest them and amuse them as best they
can during their evening's leisure. But they are inclined to
ignore the industrial life, they like to forget the grim truth that
if girls work for less than a living wage, in a vitiated atmosphere, they are not likely to become the strong, self-controlled
women whom we desire the clubs to train. They are afraid in
their club to discuss the relations of girls to boys, lest they alight
on dangerous ground. But if they are to serve their generation
and satisfy the claims of posterity on their work, they must
make their girls realize the difference between passion and love
based on spiritual affinity. The girls' club can suggest ideals
which may be developed even in the most uncongenial environment of tenement life. Club training, perhaps, achieves its best
results generally by indirect methods. But unless the leaders
do realize the most serious significance of their work, and do

acquire some industrial and sociological knowledge; unless they are willing to understand the temptations affecting the girls' lives – their efforts are likely to be capricious and their influence merely superficial.[22]

BRINGING UP JEWISH CHILDREN

We want our children to grow into good men and women, strong enough to accomplish deeds of virtue. At our peril, we neglect to give them the discipline which will lead them to the realization of God's presence, for God is the source of the highest virtue. If children once acquire the habit of worship, it is never likely to leave them, even when their lives become full of pressing cares and harassing duties and bewildering ambitions. Indeed, as years pass, they will grow more and more dependent on the power of prayer to create joy in their lives and to give them courage to overcome every difficulty and danger, which presents itself. The development of life should include the strengthening of our faith. Conduct, let us remind ourselves, is three-fourths of human life. We want our children's conduct to be influenced by the highest ideals; we them to walk humbly with their God from their earliest years. If they can once feel the influence of God's love in their lives, they will hate sin, for sin prevents them from realizing God.

In order that Judaism should be a living religion to our children, its precepts must be transmitted to them with intelligence and loving care. We can, if we will, create an atmosphere in our homes which shall be conducive to prayer and aspiration. If we venture simply and genuinely to admit our conscious dependence on God for strength and guidance in everyday life, we may inspire all the members of our household with that reverence which alone makes sincere worship possible. If we ourselves perform perfunctorily the religious obligations which we recognize in our home life, their inspiring power will disappear. They will be accomplished as tasks irksome in themselves and unrelated to other phases of our daily lives ... Children hunger for sympathy, and we can not secure their love and respect more readily than by convincing them that we, as they, are subject to temptations and determined to overcome them; that we too have knowledge of great weakness in the presence of the difficulties which our lives continually present to us, but that we have supreme faith in God's pity and loving kindness. How can we assure them of these facts more forcibly than by inviting them to pray with us? Family worship should be the most powerful link by which children may be bound to their parents and to one another ... By asking God in the presence *of our children* to bless the work of our lives, we can testify to our conception of the sacredness of work, as the duty we owe to man in the service of God.

By cherishing a knowledge of Hebrew in our homes, we are encouraging our children to appreciate their religious inheritance, for they can through Hebrew better understand the inward meaning of their sacred literature. Also the knowledge of Hebrew strengthens the bonds which unite English Jews with their co-religionists in all parts of the world. But, while recognizing the bond of language as an important factor in the religious development of the Jews, we must remember that a knowledge of Hebrew is not Judaism. It is, of course, very satisfactory when our children are good Hebrew scholars. Their learning is likely to lead them to the most useful of all studies – the study of the Bible. But, unless they have acquired the habit of prayer, unless their conduct reveals a devotion to Jewish principles, they will not be equal to the responsibilities which they have received from God. In our home services, then, we must emphasize above all things the necessity of real intelligent communion with God, and our worship must therefore include some 'made-up prayer' spoken in all simplicity, sincerity and reverence in the language most familiar to the worshippers.

We would desire to teach our children to love religious observances and to recognize their relation to modern life. This teaching means sacrifice on the part of the parents themselves. Not only have they to be careful to perform their observances in the spirit of prayer, but they must give up time for patient teaching, for answering questions, for making explanations. Children become indifferent to observances which have no meaning to them. When they are told, in answer to their questions, 'Read this', 'Be quiet', 'Go to synagogue', they lose interest in the apparently meaningless observances, and contempt creeps into their hearts. The 'throwing off' later is easy enough. If we let our children adrift in the world without giving the anchors they need on their passage through life, we incur a terrible responsibility. They will have *us* to thank for their purposeless, indifferent lives, for their weakness in times of temptation, for their degradation. We have received a great religious inheritance, and, unless we pass it on in its beauty, we are untrue to our trust. Indeed, it is right to remind ourselves every now and again of the sacrifices which our fathers made in the cause of religious education. In times of persecution, they suffered poverty and every sort of ignominy, in order that they should hand the lamp of the Lord to us in all its brightness. We have to trim the lamp somewhat in order, that its light should be seen by our generation.

If we refuse to give the lamp this attention – if, instead, we place it in a neglected corner, whence its brightness cannot fall on our lives – our children will live in darkness and see evil all their days.[23]

LIBERAL JUDAISM – A NATIONAL OR UNIVERSAL RELIGION?

We speak of Buddhism, but we do not speak of the Buddhist race. We speak of Christianity, but we cannot speak of the Christian race. We speak of Mahommedanism, but we cannot speak of the Mahommedan race. Why is this? The answer is obvious: It is because the Buddhist, Christian, and Mahommedan religions are spread over *many* races. Each of these religions began – as every religion must – among *one* race, but it soon became diffused among many races. The three religions just mentioned, because they count many races among their adherents, and because they desire to count many or even all races as their adherents, are rightly known as *universal* religions.

We speak, however, not only of Judaism, but also of the Jewish race. Why is this? Is Judaism *not* a universal religion? The answer to that last question is not wholly easy to give.

Judaism was in old times the religion of the *Jewish people* neither more nor less. This is acknowledged on all hands. It was a national religion. Now a national religion is one which has national gods and a national worship. In ancient times, as we know, men believed in many gods; the gods of one nation were not the gods of another ... If, however, a race of people begins to believe that there is only one God, how can there be a national religion any more? A national religion – which by its very definition implies special gods for a special nation – has then become an inconsistency and an anachronism. A national religion with one universal God could only mean a religion in which the one God was supposed to care specially for, or to show partial regard to, the members of one particular race. A national religion with a universal God is in some respects a worse religion than a national religion with its special and national gods.

And a national religion in this sense Judaism unquestionably is not. Neither in its Conservative nor its Liberal form does Judaism hold that God cares specially for, or shows partial regard to, the Jews. This divine partiality was indeed a trouble from which Judaism suffered in the past. But, as I have said in earlier chapters, the trouble has been completely got over. No Jew believes that the divine Father shows partiality, or that he cares for one set of his children more than for another.

On the other hand, though Judaism is not a national religion in the only right and true sense in which a monotheistic religion can justly be called a national religion, in the sense, that is, that the one God is partial, it may perhaps be called a national religion *de facto* though not *de jure*, and it may be called a national religion in a secondary sense for two special reasons.

Why, to begin with, a national religion *de facto*? Well, because, as a matter of fact, the Jewish religion is almost entirely confined to the Jewish race. We may deeply deplore the fact, but a fact is none the less a fact because we deplore it. The Jewish race – scholars have shown – is in all probability not a pure race. It has received numerous infiltrations from outside. Numerous proselytes to the religion have been, as it were, adopted into the race. Nevertheless, we can still speak of the Jewish race, even though it is not a pure race. We can still speak of the Jewish race, though many of us may hold that we cannot and should not speak of the Jewish nation.

This, then, is the reason why, *de facto*, Judaism may still be called – however much we may deplore it – a national religion. It has, men say, no adherents outside the Jewish race; and if a proselyte joins it, he or his children become absorbed into that race.

Next, what are the two reasons because of which Judaism, in a secondary sense, may be called a national religion?

The first reason is that though Judaism is emphatically a monotheistic religion, and though it believes in, and stands for, an impartial God, its outward form, its ceremonial, appears to wear a markedly national hue. It wears such a markedly national hue more especially among Conservatives, but to some extent also among Liberals. For instance, the Passover is, at first sight, a purely national festival.

Secondly – and the second reason is more important than the first – the One God is still, many persons would say, in some special sense, the God of Israel; Israel is, in some special sense, his peculiar or chosen people. God has special relations with Israel. The divine partiality, chased out of one window, seems to come back through another.

What are we to say to this? It does seem to me that, in the ordinary liturgy, traces of the old false national conception remain. And one of the duties of Liberal Judaism is so to modify the old liturgy that, without losing its historic character, all traces of the partial God, of the God who cares for, or thinks of, or values, Israel more than other races may be expunged.

But – it may be urged – the doctrine of the peculiar or chosen people is not limited to Conservative Judaism. It is also strongly maintained by Liberals. They, too, hold that God has special relations with Israel, that the Jews have a special religious vocation or mission. Does not this mean partiality? Does it not mean a national religion of an anachronistic and obsolete type?

Surely not. We hold that the special relations with Israel are not specifically for the sake of Israel, but for the sake of the world, for the sake of true religion. Certainly the special relations have never resulted in external prosperity. They have resulted in trouble and persecution and suffering, and for the majority of the Jewish race they still so result. It has been an election to sorrow and pain; a vocation to suffering and privation and woe.

Thus the 'mission of Israel' which is the only apparently national feature in Liberal–Jewish doctrine is, when rightly explained, not a national feature at all. It is a religious doctrine pure and simple, and a religious doctrine which looks outward, not inward, which thinks of others as the end and of Israel as the means.

And so if the Jews, passing out of the limited national phase, are to regard themselves, as most (I do not say all) Liberal Jews think they should regard themselves, not as a people, not as a nation, not even as a race, but as a religious brotherhood, a religious community or denomination, then Judaism is in all respects a universal and not a national religion. Its doctrine is universal: the mission of Israel becomes the mission of a brotherhood, no longer the mission of a race. The bond which holds them together is the bond of religion.[25]

THE CENTRES OF JUDAISM

The conception 'Jew' is so inextricably mixed up with religion that it is extremely difficult to free it from any religious connection. And the argument shows that there can be no compromise. There can be no *via media*. There can be no half-way house. Either the Jews must be a religious community – if you like to use the words in a non-natural sense, a priest people – and that only. Or they must be a nation, the men and women of which (like the men and women of every other modern nation) may belong to all religions or to none ...

So far, then, as Judaism is concerned, I should say that the Christian culture and conception of life contain much which is congruent to Judaism or which is essentially Jewish; that they contain some things which are supplementary and complementary to the best and highest Jewish ideas; that they contain a few things which are antipathetic to Judaism. As regards, then, the first class, there can be no objection to our assimilating it all. As regards the second, I hold that Liberal Judaism will be all the richer and truer for assimilating it. As regards the third, it can be trusted to be alive enough and strong enough to reject the food which is discordant with its own organism and unsuited to its own life. Moreover, if I read the signs of our age aright, the third class is slowly diminishing. There is much in modern culture and in the modern conception of life which is more sympathetic to Judaism than to the mediaeval conception of Christianity. On the whole, the modern conception of life tends to become not *less* Jewish, but *more* Jewish. If this statement is true, it is most important, though the proofs or illustrations of it cannot be attempted here. But it may at least be said that the whole modern European attitude to earthly life in its relation to the life after death is far more Jewish than was the prevailing attitude of Europe to that life right up to the eighteenth and nineteenth centuries. I, therefore, hold that there is little in our modern environment or 'culture' which is disintegrating to Judaism in general or to Liberal Judaism in particular, but that, on the contrary, there is much which may deepen and enrich it. To put Judaism into a corner, to remove it from Europe and America, to isolate it, to segregate its believers, would not make it grander and truer, but would impoverish and degrade it ...

There are, indeed, some who vaguely speak of, and desire, a purely *spiritual* centre. But for what end? And is there to be, and can there be, a spiritual centre without a national centre as well? Assuming, however, that there could be such a purely spiritual centre, what would be its utility and what would be its function? People speak of a Jewish university. But surely those who are touched by the modern spirit must look with considerable mistrust upon a sectarian university. What is a Jewish university to teach? Jewish chemistry? Jewish mathematics? Obviously not. Jewish history, then? Jewish philosophy? If by Jewish history is meant the history of the Jews that can be taught as well in London as in Jerusalem. But if Jewish history means history from a Jewish point of view, or if Jewish philosophy means philosophy from a Jewish point of view, surely we have got, or are getting, beyond that. In a university, history and philosophy must be taught from *no* special point of view, and certainly not from a *sectarian* point of view. In history and philosophy we must rise above the sects. Our only point of view must be truth, which can best be served from the clash of opinions in a free and wholly unsectarian university. And so, too, with the history of religion, and so, too, even with theology *as it should be pursued at a university, and not at a theological training college.* The new English universities have started free faculties of Theology and of the History of Religion. I hope there may tomorrow be a Professor of Theology who is a Jew, even as today there is a Professor of Philosophy. That is the modern tendency; that is the modern direction. Are we going to set up a Jewish university at which the direction is to be turned backwards towards mediaevalism? A Christian, a Jewish, a Mohammedan university; in the future let us hope they will all alike be contradictions in terms.

If it is desired to turn more able Jewish minds to study Jewish history and literature, to work creatively at theology and philosophy, there are other and better means than a national, or even a spiritual, centre. Create some *really* well-endowed colleges and seminaries, run on modern lines and with adequate *freedom,* and what is wanted will be achieved. To these add a *highly paid* ministry, some of whom shall be allowed to have adequate leisure to think, to read, to write.

We do not need *one* centre; we need *many* centres; not one centre, aloof from the pulse and throb of modern civilization, but many centres, planted right in its midst, yet radiating forth Jewish thought and Jewish conceptions of life from among them. For religious influence and enlightenment I would prefer a noble college in London to a university in Jerusalem. I am not sure that a spiritual centre (*if* such Rome be) is not a heritage full of difficulties for Roman Catholics; I have no desire to create one (even without a Pope) for Judaism. If, indeed, the Jewish settlements in Palestine should increase and multiply; if, whether wisely or unwisely, an autonomous Jewish state be attempted there, under the suzerainty of one of the Great Powers, it would obviously be as desirable that there should be a university in Palestine as in any other country of the world. But that this university would be of importance and help for Judaism and Liberal Judaism I do not believe. So far as it had any religious influence at all, it would be less likely to be Liberal than Ultramontane. And in Ultramontanism, whether in one religion or in another, there lies danger.

From the religious point of view, Liberal Judaism, which aims at a spiritual universalism, must deprecate the idea of being confined to the limits of a single people or of a single land. From the religious point of view, if the Jews are again to be a nation, Liberal Judaism could only accept such a solution of the so-called 'Jewish problem', if Jews can form a nation such as the English or the Italians are, a nation, that is, whose citizens can be of more religions than one.

Religion has become so integral a part of the Jew that if an attempt were made to form a new Jewish state, it would be exceedingly difficult to know how to deal with it. Nothing could be more abhorrent to the modern spirit, nothing could be more opposed to all that we have claimed and fought for, than to make religion the test of citizenship. And yet in a Jewish state what other test could there be? If ten French Christians immigrate into Palestine and live there for five or seven years, are they to be refused the rights of citizenship and naturalisation? Will they not be allowed to become Jews? If they are so allowed, how curious; if they are not so allowed, how monstrous! The truth is that the Jewish religion has made a Jewish state almost inconceivable.[26]

FAITH TODAY

Two contrasting facts stand out in the spiritual state of the modern world. One is the need for faith. The other is there are greater difficulties than ever in the way of faith. On the one hand, many feel in themselves a desire, a longing, a deep yearning, which can only be satisfied by faith; on the other hand, the thought and life of the modern world puts tremendous obstacles in its way. That is a sad state, but also a dangerous one; for unless the need is satisfied, there is a serious threat to the spiritual endowments of individuals. That in itself is vitally important. But more than the life of individuals depends upon it. The collective life of humanity is involved. The problem of social relations, the international confusion and danger of our time, the new and dangerous political creeds, all show that something is lacking in its life. If those who lack faith do not find it, not only will there be many in this world who will lack the guidance, strength and peace which it alone can give, but we also shall not get the kind of world we want, the kind of world we must have, if human life and the life of humanity are to be worth living.

Some seek to meet the need in humanity's life by organization, and others hope to overcome it by revolution, yet organization is constantly frustrated, its aims 'sicklied o'er with the pale cast' of ineffectiveness, and revolution holds no promise but of itself. They cannot satisfy humanity's need for peace and social justice. That satisfaction can come only from the spirit of man. From it issue ultimately the forces that create the moral, social and international life of the human race. The kind of world we shall have in the future will be decided by the standards, ideas and ideals which are now present in men's thoughts and aspirations; in other words, by the forces which move in the spirit of man.

Faith describes a quality, a possession, an attitude, a direction of the spirit. An adequate, or exact, definition is impossible. It is a simple word with a variety of meanings, and some of those meanings have a most complex content. It is, with some people, just simply the belief that there is a God, and the trust in him; with others, it is the name for a whole philosophy of life and the universe, which, because of its very scope, must be full of complexities. Perhaps I can express the meaning I see in it by defining it as the attitude towards the universe and life, which recognizes the presence and dominance of spirit. It describes the direction of the whole personality, thought, feeling and will. It is belief, it is trust, it is the impulse to striving, and the revealer of the goal for human endeavour; that is what I take faith in God to mean. The completeness of this attitude is called love for Him. Therefore, the essence of faith is the commandment, 'Thou shalt love the Lord thy God with all thy heart, with all thy soul and with all of thy might.' Love and trust show faith in its completeness, when the whole personality is suffused and impelled by it.[27]

THE PROBLEM OF EVIL

Looking through history, we find that there is a gradual movement towards good. Evil is very apparent. Again and again, after a period of comparative progress, there is a bad retrogression. Humanity turns to evil, and seems to lose all it has gained, and the setback is all the more lamentable as humanity has had time and opportunity to recognize spiritual good. But seen over a long period, good does ultimately prevail, and we know that it is God who triumphs over the forces of evil created by man.

If today our Jewish brotherhood would stop bothering about dogma and minute ceremonial regulations, and its own cleverness and its own worldly success, and recognize anew its religious purpose, and became once more aflame with God, then, indeed we might hope to lay the foundation on which to build up the Kingdom of God.

But supposing nothing on a grandiose scale can be achieved. There is just ourselves – the small, weak, imperfect Jew and Jewess who is passionately yearning towards God. What about it? *You* are here. You yourself mean to discover God. You may be alone with the Alone, but you have the power within yourself, and if this Sabbath is to be *real* to you, you can make the tremendous effort which will lead to your complete at-one-ment with God.

But there is perhaps a growing feeling in your heart that God to whom you prayed all the year, in whom you trusted, has let you down. So much evil has been perpetuated in this last year, as well as in all previous years; so many innocent people have suffered; so many people have missed the opportunities which should have been theirs, as part of their human birthright. Why? Why?

Friends, don't you think we are a little unreasonable in the blame we cast upon God. He, through His teachers, revealed to us thousands of years ago what would happen. He told us what would occur if we worshipped force and material success, instead of exalting the power of the spirit and seeking the paths of virtue and of love. He is renewing His word again and again to us now. Why blame Him when we went off on the track which must lead to disaster? Don't we hear Him now? Why not? Are we deafened by the shouts of savages, by the cries of lustful men, by the poisonous whispers of self indulgent women? Is it possible that we have been indifferent to the cause of righteousness, that we have ignored the claims of love and truth, of justice and mercy, so we were not properly keyed up to hear God? Let us try again. Let us speak to Him in the morning and speak to Him at night. We are so busy! We have no time for God. We are too absorbed in other things. The interference must be that other things are more important and so we come back again to the cause of the world's misery. We have been putting other values before the value of faith.

But I am assuming a great deal in suggesting that the power in your souls which guides you to righteousness is God, and that you should give yourself time, at whatever cost, morning and evening, to speak to Him when you are not doing anything else, and all through the day when you are engaged in work or in recreation, take seconds all day long, to think of God.

The experience of Jews throughout their history has brought me to this faith. They lived in the light of God. They consciously sought His guidance. They placed their lives before Him for His judgement. They themselves compared their standards with His standards and sought to make good. 'Seek the Lord at all times. Call upon Him while He is near.' Isaiah conceived that way of life, and found that it worked. 'Ye shall be holy, for I, the Lord thy God, am holy.'[28]

FAITH IN HUMANITY IN THE FACE OF EVIL

In this letter, I want to write of our relations with one another. Perhaps it would be simpler to call this part of our discussion 'Faith in Man', for if we accept the suggestion that there is something divine in human personality, we must feel reverence for every man and trust that he is 'making for righteousness'. If, however, we can, as we want to do, consider *real* life, we claim that we cannot be expected to reverence our enemies when they have proved themselves cruel and treacherous, mean and crafty. As Jews, we can, I think, nevertheless, affirm that if we had, from the beginning, shown proper faith in man, the sadistic tendencies, which lead to moral degradation, and which we notice particularly in our enemies, would never have developed.

War is a large factor in creating the evils which we deplore most at the present time, but we cannot hold our enemies altogether responsible for the war conditions. Before there was any idea or expectation of this present war, the moral and religious standard of life in every country, in every city, in every home, was far below that which belongs to those whose faith in God has led them to have faith in man. If we reverence the divine in man, we must again give him the 'large place' in which that divine element can grow. I recall with love and appreciation those words of the Psalmist: 'God has set me in a large place.' This verse does not refer to good housing and open spaces, although we know that the child's satisfactory spiritual growth does require space and privacy, light and air; the words mean, I think, that every man requires freedom. He must not be bullied or oppressed; he must be given his opportunity to develop his personality; he must not be allowed to suffer through neglect from any curable form of ignorance or disease. He must be trained to show love and kindness to his fellow men, to seek truth, and to show mercy and justice to all with whom he comes in contact.

I say that none of us has been sufficiently alive to these obligations and war is one of the evils which has ensued. How often in our prayers, we ask for the power to distinguish between good and evil. We need God's light, in order that we may see light. Nevertheless, we allowed the economic misery of the Germans to become so intense, that they could find no true deliverance, and stumbled into hailing the advent of Hitler, and thought he was their saviour.

We must believe in the divine spark in every man, and yet with shame and anxiety we must say that it may be altogether hidden by human unkindness, if evil is allowed to increase without restraint ...

We know that there is room in God's world for every type of man and woman, and they are our sisters and brothers, for we are all the children of God. We must not make life harder through our conduct for any individual we find in the world, for our faith in man which arises from our faith in God convinces us that his right to live is the same as our own. We all believe that we are working to build up a better world. That is our great hope and consolation in these days of suffering. The world can only be better when we can trust one another in our business life, our recreational life, and in our international life. It is, however, no good to try to live in a fool's paradise.

We *know* that there are crooks in business, men and women who have no appreciation of fairness in sport, governments which cannot be trusted. The time will certainly come when faith in man will be established, for God Himself, who created man in His image is a guarantee for the possibility that man can attain to trustworthiness, and if individuals can reach this stage in moral development, so assuredly must it be possible for nations.

It seems to me that the progress of the individual and of the nation depends in a large measure on man being able to complete satisfactorily a term of probation. As individuals, we must prove that we merit the confidence of God: 'Ye shall be holy, for I the Lord Thy God am holy.' In contact with God we can raise our standard of life, and this process leads to holiness. God will know if we ring true even to the inward parts. We cannot deceive Him. We must fit ourselves to become His servants and accept the fact that the process of probation will be hard and last a long time. If we deserve to be trusted by God to do His work, I believe we shall merit the confidence of man. In the world of the future, men will have the governments which reveal the stage of morality which they themselves have reached. In the past, some nations have been backward in intelligence, and had to struggle for ages before they could attain the standard of their generation. Some have been hopeless defectives and have been allowed to disappear. Perhaps the same thing must happen on the moral plane. Nations must prove their ability to reach the average standard of their time, and be willing with other nations to attain an infinitely higher stage of moral and spiritual progress. Our faith in man, based on faith in the Fatherhood of God, forbids us to despair of human progress.[29]

FAITH AND SUFFERING

Faith should not only help us in the choice and conduct of our active lives, but should also make us strong in the power of endurance. We remember that Job, when he was suffering every conceivable misery known to man, when he was bereft of all his children and his possessions, when he was being sorely tried by physical disease, became gradually conscious of the mystery of God's love and the power of faith was kindled within him. He had been rather a self-righteous man, unaware of his own spiritual needs and limitations. God, through His chastening, taught him to realize His presence. The problem of suffering and evil, continues as in the days of Job, and we have to reconcile it with the existence of an Omnipresent and perfect God. Evil exists. Therefore God allows it to exist for He is all-powerful. We cannot solve the mystery of evil. Our faith can only suggest palliatives, which render its existence more endurable. We admit that some evil is the result of wrong-doing. If we indulge in frequent uncontrolled tempers, we gradually alienate our relations and friends; if we have recourse to gambling or drinking our moral sense becomes weaker. We neglect our duties, and misery falls on ourselves and our homes. Then again we may commit some deed of treachery or impurity, beyond the reach of civil or criminal law, and conceal it so well, that the world knows nothing of it. Yet this deed will sooner or later make us suffer. We cannot escape its results. 'Be sure', says the Bible, 'that your sin will find you out.' Some people may refuse to be deterred from evil by the fear of punishment, but they cannot be altogether unaffected by the knowledge, that their children will suffer for their sakes. Surely no stronger incentive can induce men and women to lead steady, pure lives than the knowledge that, if they sin, the consequences of shame and guilt, must be shared by the beings, whom they love most in the world. Punishment which follows sin, is just and comprehensible, even to our limited human understanding. But much evil exists, which is by no means the result of sin ...

We must admit that misery and pain are awful while they last. The righteous suffer with the wicked; the innocent with the guilty. Faith faces these facts courageously and patiently. I doubt whether a man who, in the midst of an honourable, independent life, is suddenly afflicted with some horrible disease, which renders him for an indefinite period of time a burden to himself, and to his family, can derive much comfort from the hope of compensation in another world. The only real comfort in such cases must lie in the belief that there *is* some explanation for the existence of evil, for God is good. We therefore cling gratefully to our faith in immortality and believe that 'beyond the veil', in God's own good time, we shall know why the hitherto unexplained misery was allowed to exist on earth. Let us then be at peace and trust in God. Evil is no little thing; its presence is hateful to us. God bids us fight against evil and misery with all our strength, but when we can struggle no more, we have the sublime comfort of faith. God knows best, we say, and, through our tears, we look at the world and think it good.

We cannot claim that faith, however deep and sincere, can remove pain altogether. But the recognition of an omnipresent God of love gives us power to bow our heads, and to endure courageously what we cannot overcome. God loves us. So long as we live, He has work for us to do. We must take up our burdens in the spirit of David, who, when he had vainly endeavoured to save his child, ceased to mourn, and went about the work of his life. We cannot in this world understand the mystery of pain; we must believe in the God of love. He can give us peace. We must seek it from Him. Job was helped by his suffering to realize God. Our periods of suffering also, must be sent to us for our good, although in the moment of agony, we cannot help sometimes wishing that some other method of purification could have been chosen. Gradually, however, in answer to our prayers, the power of submission is vouchsafed to us. Here again, faith is justified by experience. Those of us who have suffered and have prayed, who have put our grief behind us, and let it inspire us to further effort in the cause of God, knowing that the divine help was not withheld from us. We have issued from the fire, scarred, perhaps, but stronger, nevertheless, in our love and in our faith.[30]

THE CONSEQUENCES OF FAITH

It is characteristic of the modern attitude in religion to require that its teaching and demands be related to human life. It is not enough to say to the modern man and woman, this and this is what God wants you to think, this and this is what God wants you to do, for, unlike our ancestors, we are not so certain that we know what God wants us to think, that we know what God wants us to do. Our ancestors thought they knew it, not because of intellectual conceit, but because they had a tradition, which claimed to be a revelation from God Himself. We have none. There is no book or creed of which we can say: God gave this, and it is for man only to accept it. When, then, we want to find God's will, we have to seek for it through human reason and relate it to human life. We ask of faith, even of faith in God himself, that it be related to human needs, that it have a meaning for human thought, and exercise a power on human life. What then, can faith do? Faith in its simplest of all meanings is the belief in God and trust in Him. What can it do for man? ...

The first consequence is that it overcomes the sense of emptiness. A lot has been said about the difference between our generation and the generations of the last century. There is one difference that is most significant in the present context. Whereas the Victorians felt that life was a good thing, many in our generation doubt it. Why the difference? Because our generation has become oppressed with a sense of life's emptiness. A number of different factors have made it so. The machine has taken such a big place in our existence that man has been dwarfed into insignificance. The knowledge of the universe has grown and with it the size of the universe; and man has grown smaller and smaller. Then there is the present sense of

uncertainty about the future. What can life mean to a man if
next year or the year after he may be blown out of existence in
the clash between warring nations? The future is dark and
many question whether human life, so confused, obscured,
endangered and powerless is worthwhile.

It is here that faith can do most for our present generation,
for it can bring into life a meaning which has nothing to do
with the future, which transcends man's smallness, and which
gives him a sense of human power. All the causes, the preva-
lence of the machine, the magnitude of the universe, the
uncertain future, which have created that sad and saddening
sense of emptiness oppressing our world, are thus overcome.
They draw their power not from themselves, but from a lack
within ourselves. No man doubts the meaning of his existence
who feels within himself a pulsating, aspiring life; only he feels
empty who, like the author of Ecclesiasticus, finds his own spirit
and soul shrivelled up from within, so that nothing can come
from it. The larger sense of life which faith can give overcomes
the sense of emptiness and makes life full of meaning. Why
doubt the significance of your existence and mind when in its
every moment we can experience its relation to the eternal? As
well doubt the meaning and significance of the whole universe
as to doubt the meaning of man's life. When man is aware of
the spirit in himself, he will doubt neither.

The next consequence of faith is to give guidance and strength
which we need among the difficulties and confusions of the
present world. Which way shall we go? What aims shall we
strive for? What is the right, and what the wrong, way in
human conduct? All these questions demand answers, and also
the power to carry out the answers. The experience, which we
call faith supplies the answers and gives us the power to live
up to them. Faith is a philosophy of life that is centred in
emphasis on the spiritual. Hence follows its emphasis on human
personality with its rights and responsibilities. What man means
in relation to God is the guidance it gives for living. And that
principle gives direction for political, social, economic, even
international life, and for the moral principles in personal life.
The issues between peace and war, justice and injustice in social
organization, democracy and totalitarianism, right and wrong
conduct in sexual relations, all ultimately depend for their
solution on the way man is conceived. If he is conceived as a

spiritual being, the solution will be totally different than if he is conceived as merely physical. Faith illuminates for the individual the way of life by bringing into his life the light of ultimate reality. And by binding his life to the life of the universe, it gives him the strength to follow the path it reveals, which is most often the hard way and calls for strength ...

All that faith can do is summed up in the larger experience of life which it can give to the individual man. When we love, we live more than when we do not love, because we experience more. When we enjoy art, music or literature, we live more than when we do not enjoy these things, because we experience more. The whole of life for the individual is in his experience of the universal, and the faith gives the capacity for the experience of the infinite. It, therefore, raises man above himself, giving him the strength and guidance to pursue the largest ends in his own life and in the life of humanity. All the struggles through which a man passes in his personal life, all the struggles through which humanity has passed, all have meaning and value, because these struggles have been man's effort to realize more and more in himself the infinite life and goodness in the universe. It was faith that impelled him to strive, making him something better than he was, it was faith that gave him the strength for the struggle, and it was faith that told him what the struggle means. And because we are still far from the ultimate goal and a long struggle lies before us, we need faith to beckon us on, to drive us on, and to fill our hearts with the zest of living even while we fight. By binding man to the universe faith fills man with universal life, by binding man to God faith makes man divine.[31]

A JOURNEY TO HEBRON IN 1910

Not only is Hebron one of the oldest cities in the world still inhabited, but it has been far less changed by Western influences than other famous places. Hebron is almost entirely unaffected by Christian influence. In the East, Christian influence more or less means European influence, but Hebron is still completely Oriental. It is a pity that modern travellers no longer follow the ancient route which passed from Egypt along the coast to Gaza, and then struck eastwards to Hebron. By this

route, the traveller would come upon Judea in its least modern-
ized aspect. He would find in Hebron a city without a hotel,
and unblessed by an office of the Monarch of the East, Mr Cook.
There are no modern schools in Hebron; the only institution of
the kind, the Mild-may Mission School, had scarcely any pupils
at the time of my visit. This is but another indication of the
slight effect that European forces are producing; the most
useful, so far, has been the medical mission of the United Free
Church of Scotland. But Hebron has been little receptive of the
educational and sanitary boons that are the chief good – and it
is a great good – derived from the European missions in the
East. I am almost reluctant to tell the truth, as I must, of Hebron,
and point out the pitiful plight of our brethren there, lest,
perchance, some philanthropists set about mending the evil, to
the loss of the primitiveness in which Hebron at present revels.
This is the pity of it. When you employ a modern broom to
sweep away the dirt of an ancient city, your are apt to remove
something else as well as the dirt.

Besides its low situation and its primitiveness, Hebron has a
third peculiarity. Go where one may in Judea, the ancient
places, even when still inhabited, wear a ruined look. Zion itself
is scarcely an exception. Despite its fifty thousand inhabitants,
Jerusalem has a decayed appearance, for the newest buildings
often look like ruins. The cause of this is that many structures
are planned on a bigger scale than can be executed, and thus
are left permanently unfinished, or like the windmill of Sir
Moses are disused from their very birth. Hebron, in this respect
again, is unlike the other cities of Judea. It had few big buildings, hence it has few big ruins. There are some houses of two
stories in which the upper part has never been completed, but
the houses are mostly of one story, with partially flat and partially domed roofs. The domes are the result both of necessity
and design; of necessity, because of the scarcity of large beams
for rafters; of design, because the dome enables the rain to
collect in a groove, or channel, whence it sinks into a reservoir.

Hebron, then, produces a favorable impression on the whole.
It is green and living, its hills are clad with vines, with planta-
tions of olives, pomegranates, figs, quinces, and apricots. Nowhere in Judea, except in the Jordan valley, is there such an
abundance of water. In the neighbourhood of Hebron, there
are twenty-five springs, ten large perennial wells, and several

splendid pools. Still, as when the huge cluster was borne on *two* men's shoulders from Eshkol, the best vines of Palestine grow in and around Hebron. The only large structure in the city, the mosque which surmounts the Cave of Machpelah, is in excellent repair, especially since 1894–95, when the Jewish lads from the *Alliance* school of Jerusalem renewed the iron gates within, and supplied fresh rails to the so called sarcophagi of the Patriarchs. The ancient masonry built round the cave by King Herod, the stones of which exactly resemble the masonry of the Wailing Place in Jerusalem, still stands in its massive strength.

I have said that Hebron ought to be approached from the South or West. The modern traveller, however, reaches it from the North. You leave Jerusalem by the Jaffa gate, called by the Mohammedans Bab el-Khalil, i.e., Hebron gate. The Mohammedans call Hebron el-Khalil, City of the Friend of God, a title applied to Abraham both in Jewish and Mohammedan tradition. Some, indeed, derive the name Hebron from Chaber, comrade or friend; but Hebron may mean 'confederation of cities', just as its other name, Kiriath-arba, may possibly mean Tetrapolis. The distance from Jerusalem to Hebron depends upon the views of the traveller. You can easily get to Hebron in four hours and a half by the new carriage road, but the distance, though less than twenty miles, took me fourteen hours, from five in the morning till seven at night. Most travellers turn aside to the left to see the Pools of Solomon, and the grave of Rachel lies on the right of the highroad itself. It is a modern building with a dome, and the most affecting thing is the rough-hewn block of stone worn smooth by the lips of weeping women. On the opposite side of the road is Tekoah, the birth-place of Amos; before you reach it, five miles more to the north, you get a fine glimpse also of Bethlehem, the White City, cleanest of Judean settlements. Travellers tell you that the rest of the road is uninteresting. I did not find it so. For the motive of my journey was just to see those 'uninteresting' sites, Beth-zur, where Judas Maccabeus won such a victory that he was able to rededicate the Temple, and Beth-zacharias, through whose broad valley-roads the Syrian elephants wound their heavy way, to drive Judas back on his precarious base at the capital.

It is somewhat curious that this indifference to the Maccabean sites is not restricted to Christian tourists. For, though several Jewish travellers passed from Jerusalem to Hebron in the Middle Ages, none of them mentions the Maccabean sites, none of them spares a tear or a cheer for Judas Maccabeus. They were probably absorbed in the memory of the Patriarchs and of King David, the other and older names identified with this district. Medieval fancy, besides, was too busy with peopling Hebron with myths to waste itself on sober facts. Hebron, according to a very old notion, was the place where Adam and Eve lived after their expulsion from Eden.[32]

A MEETING WITH THEODORE HERZL

On a visit to England he [Herzl] asked me for an interview, and made the request that I should become his English Zionist Lieutenant ... By every possible means, by flattery, cajolery, argument, threat, he sought to gain his end. And I admit, that so charming was the man, so powerful and winning his personality, that I had to pull myself together in order to keep straight, and to refuse him. As for his theory, it was this. He compared the Jews in the various countries to water in a sponge. A sponge can hold a certain, very limited quantity of water. Pour a little more water into the sponge, and the water trickles out at the other end. He compared the Jews in the various countries in the world to water in a sponge ... the countries of the world can endure a certain number or percentage of them. Put some more in the country what trickles out is anti-semitism. This, Herzl said, had always been. It was an iron and immutable law. The only remedy was to get all the Jews, over and above the permissible percentage, away into a country of their own. As Herzl put it, it seemed to me at the moment, sadly convincing. But then I reflected: 'Not so: at least the percentage must vary greatly in different countries, and, then, is nothing to be allowed for any progress in toleration, in understanding, in appreciation, in good-will? Must these hatreds continue for ever?' So I rejected the defeatist, sponge theory, and I reject it still ...

On the Jewish side, the Mandate led to an enormous increase and development of Jewish nationalism; on the gentile side, to an increase in anti-Semitism, and an increasing misapprehension and denial of the old Jewish position – of my once ordinary, now, alas, die-hard position ...

You see before you a disillusioned old man, a sad and embittered old man. But yet, not a hopeless old man, for he still believes in God. He refuses to bow the knee to the fashionable Zionist Baal. He refuses to succumb to Jewish nationalism, on the one hand, or to Gentile anti-Semitism on the other, even though these powerful forces so powerfully react upon, and stimulate one another. He is an extremist, a die-hard, a fanatic, if you will, but he has not lost his faith. His old ideal of the Englishman of the Jewish faith shall yet, as he believes, prevail.[33]

ANTI-SEMITISM

My slogan, 'The Englishman of the Jewish faith' is the solution of anti-Semitism and the answer to it. Such a person is a reality, and in no wise a baneful reality. It is for Jews, in spite of all temporary discouragements, to stick to the slogan through thick and thin. It is their one salvation; their charter; their watchword. It is for Christians to make it possible. It is for Christians to show their desire to be Christians by helping to cure any faults among some Jews with Christian charity, and by not helping to increase and intensify them with hatred, persecution and wrong. It is for Jews to remember that we carry, each one of us, the reputation of the entire brotherhood in the conduct of every individual; that minorities are necessarily marked out for observation and criticism, so that to escape a whipping, even if only a whipping of words, we should not merely be as good as the majority, but better. Our honour, the happiness of our religious brotherhood, the Sanctification of the Holy Name of God, whose witness we dare claim to be, should be our encouragement and our stimulus.

For countries with racial and national minorities, such as Poland and Romania, the problem is more difficult. In these countries Jews tend to be regarded, and to regard themselves, as racial minorities, as sub-nationalities. I have desired to avoid Jewish polemical questions as far as possible, but I cannot entirely conceal my considered and deliberate opinion that Jewish nationalism, or any Jewish consciousness of Jewish nationalism, in the countries of the west, Holland, France, Italy, Germany, England and America, is an evil, not unconnected with anti-Semitism, and inimical to its mitigation and disappearance. In countries such as Poland and Romania, the best one can hope for is, I fancy, two distinct patriotisms or national consciousness's, one smaller and one larger, one Jewish and one Polish, one Jewish and one Romanian. The parallel might be the two national consciousness's of a Welshman or a Scot, one for Wales or Scotland, and one for the United Kingdom. It is not an entirely satisfactory solution, but it seems to be the best in the circumstances, and it is no use blinking one's eyes to facts, whether one likes the facts or no.

One last word about religion. In medieval days religion was, as I have said, the primary cause of the hatred of the Jew. When the Crusaders waded to their knees in Jewish and Mussulmen blood through the streets of Jerusalem, killing every man, woman and child in their wild lust for slaughter, it was done in the cause and in the name of Christianity and of religion. Things are different now. Religious hatred has not wholly ceased, but it is generally secondary. And we may go further, and say that the trouble now is, not the Jew who believes in Judaism and practises it, whether he be Orthodox or Liberal, not even the Jew who, though by stress of doubt religiously agnostic, is yet of high moral excellence and spirituality, but the Jew who disbelieves in, and is hostile to, religion altogether. The atheistic, Bolshevist Jew supplies anti-Semitism with priceless fuel, nor can we say that the attack however exaggerated – and however easily to be explained, is yet entirely without justification. The solution lies in Jewish hands. Orthodox Jews will say it lies in Orthodox Judaism. Liberal Jews will say that it lies in Liberal Judaism. Perhaps for many generations it may lie in both. In any case, it is for Jewish parents, whether Orthodox or Liberal, to do their utmost to prevent the increase of the atheistic, antireligious Jew. He is without value; he has no meaning; he is a danger. He breeds anti-Semitism; the least worthy and the least unjustifiable anti-Semitism is caused by him.[34]

THE PROBLEMS FACING LIBERAL JUDAISM

Judaism is assailed today by many forces. These forces are of considerable power. The forces are not the same as the forces which assailed it in olden days, but they are, perhaps, more insidious, more seductive, more *dissolvent*. In the old days the religious power of Judaism was, we might say, assailed by the religious power of the Church, of Christianity. It was a case of one religious power assailed by another, a little power assailed by a big power. And that direct assailing made the little power more resolved to resist; it stiffened its back; it braced its resolve. Judaism is no longer assailed by the Church. Indeed, the Church and ourselves are now, to a large extent, allies instead of enemies, allies in a defense against assaults of a common enemy or enemies. The direct assaults of Christians against Judaism through the missionary societies whether Protestant or Catholic, are comparatively negligible. There is, indeed, a certain indirect pressure in countries such as England or America where the Jews, a small minority amid a huge majority, are free and unpersecuted. There is a certain inevitable gravitation towards the religion of the majority. Inter-marriages are not infrequent, and their result is usually, though not invariably, disadvantageous to the minority. But this danger, too, is of no great importance, and, as a tremendously keen advocate of the Judaism of the so-called Diaspora, I would add that the danger is well worthwhile, and richly compensated for by its enormous advantages. The forces I am alluding to are very different, and they are mainly modern and new.

There is, first of all, the force of religious indifference. It is a strange force. The very fact that we are here in this building this afternoon shows that we are not *entirely* indifferent. Nevertheless, indifference is a force which, partly through its many causes, is not only powerful, but very contagious and seductive. It has a strong ally, as well as a partial cause, in that inertia or laziness to which so many of us are subject …

Then there is a second force, rather difficult to describe. It takes two forms. Its first form is what is known as a dislike of, an objection to, all institutional religion. To this objection I would wish to be quite fair. It is sometimes perfectly honest, and may be due to causes for which institutional religion (which, as we all know, may be very unattractive) is itself to blame. Sometimes it is, I fear, only an elegant cloak or mask for indifference. But whatever its cause, and whatever its degree of sincerity, it is a danger to our movement. The Jew and Jewess who hold themselves aloof from all institutional religion are, in most cases, bound to become alienated from Judaism. For Judaism, like other religions, is partly dependant upon a corporate, public and institutional life, and the more that life is weakened, and the feebler it becomes, the more will the religion tend to wither and fade away. I may add that even for the individual's own private religious life and vitality, there are only very few highly gifted and exceptional souls who, without danger or stunting, can do without institutional religion; but I ask you to think not so much of the loss to the individual, as the loss to the community and to the cause.

Another form which this second danger takes is this. There are those who say: 'A *particular* religion is too narrow a religion. One can be deeply religious,' they urge, 'and yet, for that very reason, be attached neither to synagogue nor church.' It would take me too long to deal with that argument and danger; I believe it to be sophistical; but, obviously, those who take this line are useless as Jews, whether to Orthodoxy or to Liberalism. I must, however, say a word about a precisely opposite danger. There are those whose Judaism is confined to, and only shows itself in, an almost fanatical opposition to, and dislike of, Christianity. What good is this? It may, indeed, suffice to keep them, as people say, within the Jewish fold, and our cemeteries may be assured of receiving their bodies, but the enrichment of the cemetery is preceded by the impoverishment of the religion. If ever there was a negative and futile sort of religion it is one the only manifestation of which is the dislike of another religion than your own. It is easy, but cheap; it is simple, but useless. Judaism can only be preserved by the positive affection, by the *positive* service, by the *positive* devotion, of its members; mere negative dislike of our neighbour's religion is of no value whatever. To be above creeds and distinctions is dangerous; to be so below your creed that you can only be described as *not* something else is both dangerous and despicable.

A third or fourth danger is much larger and more ominous. You must all be aware of it. It affects our Christian neighbours quite as much as it affects ourselves. A great attack is going on against Theism – that is, against the sort of God, the Father and King, whom Judaism and Christianity alike dare to believe in, to proclaim, and to worship – and also against all religion. Theism is on its defence; it is on its defence against Pantheism, or against an impersonal and un-self-conscious God; religion as a whole is on its defence. We are living in the midst of these attacks. We cannot ignore them ...

I have to speak now of yet another danger, or rather of two dangers, which I will compress into a very few words. Orthodox Judaism has two sides, each of which should support and strengthen the other. But as things now are in England both are being weakened at one and the same time, and hence the decay of each is hastened and increased by the decay of the other. I refer to Orthodox Jewish belief and Orthodox Jewish practice. As regards belief, Orthodox Judaism depends upon the doctrine of the Mosaic origin, the homogeneity, the perfection and verbal inspiration of the Pentateuchal laws. But that doctrine historic investigation, biblical criticism and the philosophy of religion, make it increasingly difficult to maintain. As regards practice, with the weakening of the doctrine, which is the basis of the practice, the exigencies of modern life put increasing difficulties in the way. Few among us would wish the Jews to live in a segregated ghetto; few would wish them not to take their share in the general life, and in the general culture, of England, their home. One point more; I will mention a highly contentious word, but yet I will avoid everything which is contentious. I name the word Zionism. Now our movement is neutral as regards Zionism. We have among us eager and enthusiastic advocates, and eager and enthusiastic opponents, of Zionism. But what I want to say is this. Even in Palestine, even in the very seat and living centre of Zionism, many of the difficulties which assail Judaism *here* assail it *there*. Some possibly assail Judaism with even greater power in Palestine than in England. And many earnest Zionists would tell you that if the growing number of Jews in Palestine is to grow up, not a godless and religionless, but a God-fearing and God-loving, community – a community which, in all sincerity and passion, can still call upon *Aveenu Malkaynu*, our Father, our King, then it must be some form (and the form is comparatively indifferent) of Liberal Judaism which will save them, some form of Liberal Judaism which must become their religion.[35]

DRIFTING AWAY FROM JUDAISM

Most Jews who drift from Judaism drift into nothingness, whether their faith has the name of any existing creed, or is too indefinite even to be named. Moreover, just as we cannot become Christians merely by ceasing to be Jews, so we are not Jews merely because we are not Christians. We have to realize our inheritance and let it influence our lives, otherwise only the noblest souls among us can steer clear of materialism. And the materialism of Jews is of the lowest and most gross order, perhaps because the height, from which they descended, is so glorious in its possibilities. We can only arrest this descent, by ourselves climbing nearer the heights, and proving by the joyousness of our lives, that we realize the blessings of Judaism. Thus, too, and thus only, can we arrest the departure of those truly religious members of our brotherhood, who leave our community, because its forms and ceremonies offer them so little spiritual satisfaction ... We must by our efforts re-trim the lamp of Judaism and cause it to shine with a beautiful, pure light, which cannot be extinguished.

As Jews, we believe our religion to be based on irrefutable principles. Any defection from our community, we regard not only as a loss to ourselves, but as an injury to the proselyte. It is well with us as Jews. We are conscious of the Omnipresence of God. We feel the influence of His love. We obtain strength from our direct communion with Him.

It is our mission to draw men within our brotherhood. We dare not let them pass away, without making an effort to reclaim them. Moreover, at this moment it would seem that our mission is drawing nearer to its accomplishment.

For, passing from other faiths, we believe that men are gradually coming to worship the God of Israel, and to recognize the unity of His being and the law of righteousness, which He has established. Even now we see a gradual approximation of men of all creeds. The Trinitarian idea is accepted with intellectual reservations by believing Christians. The conception of three Entities, seems to be merging into the recognition of different attributes in the one Divine Being.

Christian divines insist more and more on personal responsibility in the conduct of life. The universal Fatherhood is being so much better understood that the doctrine of everlasting punishment for the unbaptised, is being discredited. Then, again, other communities are coming into existence on purpose to minister to the one God, and to worship Him simply and directly by prayer, and by works of righteousness. These new Churches recognize most of our 'principles', and we consequently feel in close sympathy with them. All these signs of the times awaken our gratitude and stimulate our trust in the God of truth; they affect our religious obligations by strengthening them, for the faith which inspires us is now being quickened by hope. It sometimes occurs, in the history of scientific discoveries, that two men, working under different conditions, in opposite parts of the globe, alight on the same truth by different methods. The truth of the discovery is not for this reason less valued; rather is it doubly proved. Similarly, our devotion as Jews to Judaism is strengthened, when we find that some of the constituent elements of our faith, are being received more and more favourably by sister religions.

The general approximation of different communities can be facilitated in two ways, and both are surely desirable, because universal religious brotherhood will put an end to religious strife, the most bitter of all forms of human strife. In the first place, we can study the doctrines of other faiths with reverence and respect, and we shall find among them some developments of Jewish dogma, which will help us in our search after God. We can gratefully adopt such teaching, as is consistent with the principles of Judaism to which we subscribe …

The second method of approximation is by increased loyalty to the fundamentals of our own faith, for thus we shall draw other communities nearer to ourselves. After all, the new theistic communities and the developments of old communities are new, and we as Jews have for our faith the most precious of all testimonies – the unbroken testimony of past generations. Our religion possesses all the picturesqueness, warmth, colour, poetry and romance which belongs to antiquity. Conduct based on the teaching of Judaism may attain to the sublime, and our lapses are due not to inherent defects in our faith, but to inherent defects in ourselves. The new organizations look to us for spiritual light. That light must be found burning with ever-increasing brightness in our own lives, and in the corporate life of our community. By loyalty to our own faith, and by reverent appreciation of the faith of other men, we shall help to establish the dominion of the God of love throughout the world.[36]

THE PUZZLING PROGRESSION OF HUMANITY

Liberal Judaism declares and believes that the course of human history is, in spite of set-backs, a divinely intended course of progress from ignorance to knowledge, from savagery to civilisation, from crude and low ideas about goodness to purer and nobler ideas, from superstition and cruelty to enlightenment and compassion. What some people call development, and others call evolution, we accept as the deliberate will of the divine Ruler. The development or evolution is the deliberate will.

We know that this progress has been terribly slow, and that it has been accompanied, so far as we can judge, by serious setbacks and by appalling waste. Comparatively civilised nations have been ruined by savages and barbarians; and many barbarous and savage races have never developed into civilisation at all; while recent investigation has shown us that human history is far older than used to be supposed, and that, therefore, the development of righteousness and of the knowledge of God has been painfully and puzzlingly slow ...

Why all this long development? Why all this apparent waste? Why all this long painful history of slow movement from animal to lowest savage, and from lowest savage to civilization?

We do not know. We cannot tell. Still it is, I think, much more cheering and comforting to believe that man has slowly risen than to believe (as has been widely believed) that he suddenly fell. A slow ascent fits in better with our conception of God than a sudden fall. An enduring golden age in a far-distant future is a more comforting and bracing idea than a transitory golden age in a far-distant past. There is comfort, too, in the very thought that human nature has in it the power to grow and improve, and to reach ever nearer – by whatever gradual stages – to the perfect ideal. It makes us think more and not less of human nature when we realise that in some early savage there was a germ of a Socrates or an Isaiah.[37]

THE MISSION OF ISRAEL

A chosen people: a consecrated brotherhood. Chosen for others, and not for themselves. But if chosen for others, chosen with a certain end and purpose: hence, we may equally well say, invested with a special mission, a peculiar calling ...

That the Jews have any religious work still to do is a doctrine largely limited to the Jews themselves, and I fully admit that it is a daring thing to hold to a doctrine which is rejected by a very large majority of the civilised world. Still we must not be frightened at being in a minority. We may, nevertheless, in the long run, find the truth we champion more and more generally acknowledged.

Why do we still believe in the continuing and unaccomplished mission? For several reasons. Mainly, I think, because our religion and our religious experience have not yet become the religion and religious experience of mankind, and we possess the faith that in their essentials they are destined to become so. If it be said: 'Even if your religion is to become in its essentials the religion of mankind, what are you doing, and what do you expect to do, towards the diffusion of it?' – then I would answer: 'I am not sure that we are doing nothing now; still less am I sure that we shall do nothing in the future. They too may serve their mission who, even for long stretches of time (and to our Master a thousand years are as a day), only stand, and suffer, and wait.'

We, believe, moreover, in our general mission because of our history and because of the general history of mankind. We hold that the preservation of the Jewish race from AD 30 to AD 1912 is not due to chance, and that it has not been effected without the will and intention of God. We venture, in all humility to suppose that the purpose of this preservation is religious; that is to say, we hold that the preservation of our race and brotherhood has some religious object. In other words, the religious work which the Jewish brotherhood has to do for the world did not cease at the birth of Christianity. For my part I share these opinions. That Christianity was intended by God to play a great religious part in the world, I firmly believe, but I also believe that its appearance in the world did not betoken the end of Judaism as a religion of value. Christianity itself seems to Jews only a stage in the preparation of the world for a purified, developed, and universalised Judaism ...

In its deeper essentials then – in its conception of God and his unity, of his relation to man and of man's to him, of the true service of God and of the consecration of life – Judaism, as we believe, stands at the head of God's religions in value and truth, and these deeper essentials have not yet been wholly adopted by the world, or even by that large section of the world with which we, in England, are immediately concerned. Our special conceptions of God and of his relation to man have, in some respects, still to make their way.[38]

THE FUTURE

The future will do justice both to the protest of the Jew and to the new outlook upon religion and life which Jesus introduced to the world. For, on the one hand, thought and criticism alike are tending to the recognition of the fundamental Jewish doctrine, which Jesus like every Jew believed in and taught. God is One, and no man is God. What the Jews have died in thousands to protest against was not the teaching of Jesus, but the teaching of the Church – the incarnation, the Trinity, the worship of the Man-God, the mediation of the Messiah, the worship of the virgin, the doctrine of transubstantiation and so on. And when some liberal Protestant German theologians, of today, who are practically Unitarians, though they do not call themselves by that name, write about Rabbinism and Judaism with disdain and disapproval, they forget that what they directly depreciate and contemn, they indirectly justify and exalt. They abandon, as not originally or specifically Christian, all those doctrines against which, from the very birth of Christianity the Jews rebelled and protested. *They have come round to our position.* For surely, as regards their conception of God and His relation to the world, the orthodox Christian of every age would dub them Judaizers and heretics. If their conceptions of Christianity conquer and prevail, great is the victory of Judaism ...

Nevertheless, Jesus marks an era. It is true that much is associated with his name, which need not be associated with it. To us, when we open the New Testament and read the parable of the prodigal son, there is no novelty in it. To us, too, God is the loving Father, who yearns to forgive the penitent. If any one can read the Rabbinic teachings on repentance and deny that this is so, he must be case-hardened in prejudice. Moreover, we all know what we ourselves were taught. We were taught this doctrine, and we are not taught it from the New Testament or in connection with the name of Jesus. But, for all that, Jesus marks an era. I cannot conceive that a time will come when the figure of Jesus will no longer be a star of the first magnitude in the spiritual heavens, when he will no longer be regarded as one of the greatest religious heroes and teachers whom the world has seen. I cannot conceive that a time will come when 'the Bible' in the eyes of Europe will no longer be composed of the Old Testament and the New, but of the Old Testament only, or when the Gospels will be less prized that the Pentateuch, or the Books of Chronicles preferred to the Epistles of Paul.

The religion of the future will be, as I believe, a developed and purified Judaism, but from that developed and purified Judaism the records which tell, however imperfectly, of perhaps its greatest, as certainly of its most potent and influential teacher, will not be excluded. The roll-call of its heroes will not omit the name of Jesus. Christianity and Judaism must gradually approach each other. The one must shed the teachings which Jesus did not teach, the other must acknowledge, more fully, more frankly than has yet been done, what he did was for religion and for the world.[39]

AN AUTOBIOGRAPHICAL NOTE BY LILY MONTAGU

I came from a home in which Judaism was a reality. I was one of ten children, and we all were taught to order our lives around our religious observances. Our parents did that. My father's public and private life was directly influenced by his interest in Judaism as he conceived it. The accomplishment of his work, his form of entertainment, his personal sacrifices, expressed his faith. My mother supported the sane conceptions, but recognized that in the set of Jewish society in which we moved, we were in the minority. My father saw all around him the lax Jews, and considered them dead leaves which would drop off, and the faithful would remain and pass on true religion to the next generations.

I began to worry about the so-called dead leaves. Through the children's services held at the New West End Synagogue, I saw how the children of these same people responded to a different presentment of Judaism and rekindled the interest of their parents.

Dr Montefiore was prepared to stand by my side, as he said,

and naturally he became our leader. He and Dr Israel Abrahams and others helped us through their scholarship and deep personal faith. After the first meeting in February 1902, in the house of my sister, Mrs Franklin, that sister who from the beginning right up to the present day has helped me with her kindness and sympathy to find the right values in our work and to bring others to the same understanding, we organized the Jewish Religious Union for the Advancement of Liberal Judaism.

I saw all around me how men and women were dropping Judaism because it seemed out of date and did not belong to their lives, and I had been shown by Dr Montefiore that they had not understood the meaning of their inheritance. They must be called back. The JRU was formed, and we, a handful of men and women, faced and survived the abuse and unkindness of those who thought that we were causing schism when we started Sabbath afternoon services in the Wharncliffe Rooms. My father and other Jewish leaders regarded our efforts at the beginning with benevolent tolerance. So long as we did not interfere with the times of the existing services, we could not do much harm, and might draw in some of the waverers who never attended real services. Moreover, a Jewish movement initiated by a woman could not be of serious importance anyhow.

But people flocked to the services, and gradually it became necessary to explain through a manifesto the meaning of our presentment, how it was derived from the teaching of the prophets and that it was in harmony with the best thought of the age.

I am not going to tell the rest of the story in detail. I will only dwell on the highlights.

The JRU existed for ten years before our Rabbi came. I cannot tell you how often during that period we had solemn meetings to discuss the possibility of going on or the advisability of giving up for the time being. At one moment we thought of joining the Reform Synagogue, but we found that we should have to compromise; our presentment of Judaism would be sacrificed to convenience. By then our great following had dispersed after the fascinating novelty of our services had passed. The Orthodox lay leaders who had helped us at the beginning to arrange supplementary services found their official consciences no longer allowed them to support us. They must forget their personal predilections. We had found it necessary to establish a Synagogue and were worshipping regularly in the small building in Hill Street. Worse and worse, we were looking for our own cemetery and so would, in competition with themselves, soon be able to offer the most acceptable amenities to a large section of Orthodox supporters. Even the generously minded Orthodox Rabbis who had already risked much by cooperating with us withdrew, one by one ...

Through the desire to share with others what had been given to me, I asked Dr Montefiore and Dr Mattuck to help me to start the World Union For Progressive Judaism. I knew that in every country there were Jews who would join us in our struggle against materialism. There were splendid Liberal organizations much older than ours in Germany and in America. Some of their leaders had already helped us to establish our English Union. Now the time had come for us to work together and to found new congregations in different parts of the world and to strengthen existing ones till we became a great spiritual creative force with world responsibilities.

So we began this international religious work in 1926 through my belonging to this Synagogue and working under our leaders, and under Dr Mattuck's guidance I have carried on for 25 joyous years.

I had always wished that I could be a Minister. There was a time when for that reason, and that reason alone, I wished I had been a man. For many years, in spite of one or more timid suggestions from our colleagues, the thought of a woman reading or preaching was considered altogether improper. I even remember our dear Dr Israel Abrahams saying to me on the Eve of a Day of Atonement Service when an important reader had been taken ill: 'Why on earth are you not a man?' And we both had to agree that evidently God had not planned that I should take part in leading a service.

In 1915 Dr Mattuck recommended that I should preach at the LJS That recommendation coming from our leader and probably just at the right moment received almost unanimous approval even from those who a few years earlier thought my appearance on the Synagogue pulpit would have been dangerous. That day in June 1915 on which I spoke on 'Kinship with God' was a day of supreme happiness to me. Of course, I wished I could study and be a real Rabbi. If I had gone to Dr Mattuck then and asked him if he thought I might become a Rabbi, he might have said: 'Well, there is nothing really against it,' and being a very sagacious man, he would have added: 'Don't you think it would be better for you to qualify as a dressmaker?' But I was twenty years too old anyway.

In 1928, I dared to found a Congregation in the West Central district in connection with my Club and Settlement. Those members who formed the nucleus have remained faithful, though after 22 years the Congregation is an independent organization most of whose members have no connection with the Club. Here I have had the opportunity I longed for in a lay capacity, and my work was recognized when in November 1944, I with a group of others was officially inducted as Lay Minister. I don't know whether the other Lay Ministers felt the same exalted joy over this appointment as I did, but my glow has not cooled off even yet.[40]

NOTES

1. Claude Montefiore, *The Old Testament and After*, London: Macmillan (1923), pp. 588–90.
2. Israel Mattuck, *The Essentials of Liberal Judaism*, London: Routledge & Sons (1947), pp. 168–70.
3. Montefiore, *The Old Testament and After*, pp. 586–8.
4. Ibid., pp. 555–9.
5. Claude Montefiore, *The Jewish Religious Union: Its Principles and Future*, London: JRU (1909), pp. 9–10.
6. Mattuck, *The Essentials of Liberal Judaism*, pp. 135–8.
7. Lev. 19:18: 'Do not seek revenge or bear a grudge against one of your people, but love your neighbour as yourself. I am the Lord.' Lev. 19:19: 'Keep my decrees. Do not mate different kinds of animals. Do not plant your field with two kinds of seed. Do not wear clothing woven of two kinds of material.'
8. 'The Justification of Liberal Judaism', *Papers for Jewish People*, London: JRU (1910), pp. 19–20..
9. Lily Montagu, Archives, LJS.
10. Lily Montagu, Archives, LJS.
11. Claude Montefiore, *Liberal Judaism*, London: Macmillan, pp. 135–9.
12. Montefiore, *The Old Testament and After*, pp. 164–6.
13. 'At that time Jesus said, "I praise you, Father, Lord of heaven and earth, because you have hidden these things from the wise and learned, and revealed them to little children. Yes, Father, for this was your good pleasure. All things have been committed to me by my Father. No one knows the Son except the Father, and no one knows the Father except the Son and those to whom the Son chooses to reveal him. Come to me,

all you who are weary and burdened, and I will give you rest. Take my yoke upon you and learn from me, for I am gentle and humble in heart, and you will find rest for your souls. For my yoke is easy and my burden is light.'

14. Montefiore, *Liberal Judaism*, pp. 177–81.
15. Israel Mattuck, *Essentials of Liberal Judaism*, pp. 147–50.
16. Israel Abrahamson, *The Book of Delight*, Philadelphia: JPS (1912), pp. 242–5.
17. Montefiore, *The Old Testament and After*, pp. 560–1.
18. Lily Montagu, Archives, LJS.
19. Lily Montagu, 'The Girl in the Background', in E. J. Urwick, *Studies of Boy Life in Our Cities*, London: J.M. Dent (1904), pp. 233–54.
20. Lily Montagu herself.
21. Lily Montagu, Archives, LJS.
22. Montagu, 'The Girl in the Background', pp. 248–50.
23. Lily Montagu, *Thoughts on Judaism*, London: R. Brimley Johnson (1904), pp. 70–5.
24. Montagu, *Thoughts on Judaism*, pp. 70–5.
25. Claude Montefiore, *Outlines of Liberal Judaism*, London: Macmillan (1912), pp. 293–7.
26. Montefiore, *Liberal Judaism and Hellenism* (1937), pp. 310–25.
27. Israel Mattuck, *Faith and the Modern World*, London: JRU, pp. 3–4.
28. Lily Montagu, Archives, LJS.
29. Lily Montagu, Archives, LJS.
30. Montagu, *Thoughts on Judaism*, pp. 12–31.
31. Mattuck, *Faith and the Modern World*, pp. 16–21.
32. Abrahamson, *A Book of Delight*, pp. 62–77.
33. L. Cohen, *Some Recollections of Claude Montefiore*, London: Faber and Faber (1940), pp. 226–7.
34. Montefiore, 'Anti-Semitism' (unpublished sermon), Archives, LJS (1925).
35. Lily Montagu, Archives, LJS.
36. Montagu, *Thoughts on Judaism*, pp. 144–8.
37. Montefiore, *Outlines*, pp. 115–17.
38. Ibid., pp. 163–5.
39. Claude Montefiore, *The Synoptic Gospels*, Vol. 2, London: Macmillan (1910), pp. 162–3.
40. Lily Montagu, Archives, LJS.

Appendix: The Spiritual Possibilities in Judaism Today[1]

The history of a community, like the history of an individual, is marked by the recurrence of periods of self-consciousness and self-analysis. At such times its members consider their aggregate achievements and failures, and mark the tendencies of their corporate life. Perhaps even, the sudden recognition of facts, which have been unconsciously suppressed, may lead to regeneration. For many years self-consciousness has been growing among English Jews, and they have expressed, in whispers to one another, dissatisfaction with their spiritual state. It requires, however, some stirring accident like the Conference on Religious Education held in June last, and the East End meetings resulting from it, to cause an effective diagnosis to be made. Until Jews are honest enough to recognize that the majority of them are either devoted to ceremonialism at the expense of religion, or indifferent both to ceremonialism and to religion; until they have energy to examine their religious needs and courage to formulate them, they are courting comfort at the expense of truth, and they must fail to restore to Judaism its life and the endless possibilities inherent in life.

It is not enough for us to give a frightened glance of recognition at our materialism and spiritual lethargy, and then seek to draw the veil in all speed, hoping impotently that grim facts will grow less grim if left alone. We have ultimately to confess that facts cannot be thus set aside by mere desire. Moreover, these facts prove on examination to be stimulating rather than terrifying, fraught with hope rather than with negation. If I appear dogmatic in my efforts to prove my contention that Judaism has been allowed by the timid and the indifferent to lose much of its inspiring force, I can only plead in excuse the sincerity of my convictions.

I take as the objects of my criticism the two most comprehensive types of English Jews and for purposes of convenience call them 'East End Jews' and 'West End Jews' respectively. It must, however, be clearly understood that these two forms of religion do not prevail exclusively in any particular district of London. Representatives of both classes may sometimes live in the same house, and may, conceivably, belong to the same family. Again, a considerable district in West Central London is largely inhabited by 'East End Jews', and many 'West End Jews', with their vague ineffective aspirations, crowd the neighbourhood of Bishopsgate. But these epithets are intended to convey the idea of two sets of people, differing less in dogmatic belief than in the tone and temper of their minds, and especially in their view of the proper relations between religion and life. It will also be shown that, although these two classes are to-day quite unsympathetic to one another there are many signs of a better mutual understanding among members of the younger generation; and it is chiefly upon this reunion that I base my own belief in the possibilities of the reanimation of Judaism as a religious force. In my endeavour to rouse the lethargic I may perhaps have dwelt more fully on the defects of my two types than on their qualities, but I have little doubt that there will be many both able and willing to make the balance more even.

The 'East End Jew', whose religion is vigorous in spite of its deformities, has no confidence in the shadowy faith of the 'West End Jew', and refuses to be taught by 'West End' methods. Examining this distrust, I find that it arises from the recognition of the dissimilarity in the two religions. The 'East End Jew' is determined to follow the worship of his fathers, and spurns the flaccid religion of his 'West End' brothers. To the pious 'East End Jew' religion is obedience glorified into a cult; for him, God exists as a just Law-giver, ready to forgive and help those who obey the Law, delivered by him to his people through his servant Moses, and having misfortune and failure in reserve for the rebellious and indifferent. He is continuously conscious of the 'God without', whom he seeks to approach at prescribed times and seasons. Every act of obedience tends to increase the sum of his righteousness; no evil can touch him while pursuing the divine mandate. He does not consciously strive to realize the God and to develop it by communion with the divine Ideal of Truth and Love existing without, for the idea of an immanent divine presence does not seem to affect his creed. When he repeats the prayers ordered by his fathers, he is less stirred by the effort of the soul to hold communion with the Infinite than by a sense of righteousness resulting from unquestioning obedience. The glow, which this obedience produces, suffuses his daily life, and encourages him to persevere in his rigid observances, and to face all earthly difficulties with courage and hope. Can we wonder that the 'East End Jew' regards with half-scornful fear the man who, while still calling himself 'Jew', ventures to neglect the ordinances prescribed of old, and makes no apparent sacrifice in the cause of his faith? For him, prosperity seems to authorize self-indulgence and laxity of conduct.

Admitting the possibility that prejudice and ignorance render the 'East End' observer unappreciative in his criticism, can we substantiate for the 'West End Jew' any claim to a deeply religious life? Can we deny that in many 'West End' homes, callousness takes the place which religion should occupy? Having been born Jews, and believing it more respectable to be identified with some religion, the members of the class under consideration generally belong to some synagogue, and perhaps attend the services more or less regularly. But their religion is seldom interesting, never absorbing to them. They are far more concerned in the length of the service than in its adequacy to satisfy their spiritual needs. They make no demand on their Judaism; it has no real influence over them. They either sink into materialism or create a religion of their own, based on a vague belief in the existence of a higher law, and nourished by an exacting moral sense which requires self-restraint and self-development. This religion, without an historical past and admitting of no outward embodiment, is helpful only to those individuals whose moral strength is great enough to call it into existence. The vast majority of men and women need a more definite cult to draw them to their God. The strict system of religious discipline adopted in the 'East End' has much definite and salutary influence. It awakens veneration and instigates self-sacrifice; it leads to morality, sobriety and strength of purpose. It encourages kindly intercourse between men, inducing often heroic acts of charity. I only venture to criticize it, because I see it worshipped as God alone should be worshipped; because true communion with God is being shut off from man by the observances, which were intended to lead man to God.

Even the recent remarkable gatherings of working Jews, bent on Sabbath observance, do not allay our apprehension for the future of Judaism. While admiring the earnestness which inspired these meetings, it is to be feared that the Sabbath, instead of being desired as a day for the renewal of spiritual life, or as a stimulus to moral progress, is now required for mere physical rest and idleness, and for the complete equipment of the ritual-god, which has been fashioned so curiously and is so generally worshipped. Indeed I tremble for the future of Judaism, as I recall the words that Isaiah addresses, in the name of the Lord, to the idolaters of all ages: 'Your new moons and your appointed feasts my soul hateth: they are a trouble unto me; I am weary to bear them' (Isa. 1:14).

Between the worship of ritual prevalent in the 'East End', inspiring by its intense fervour, but repelling through the materialism and intolerance which it produces, and the vague religion of the ' West End', existing apparently but to satisfy a convention, there seems indeed little affinity. Yet the children of both types of Jews are united by a common need which neither form of religion is able to satisfy. For the sons of the pious 'East End Jew' are also beginning to question the meaning and value of the laws which bind their fathers' lives so closely. We see them shocked by their inconsistency, and disappointed, by their inadequacy; we see them drifting away from the worship which, at least in its origin, was inspiring, and, for want of some better object, devoting themselves to 'self'. The daughters of the pious do not even attend the synagogue services, which have begun to weary their brothers. Through force of habit they cling to the domestic side of religion, but they do not attempt to ennoble the sordid elements in their lives by trying to introduce the ideal.

Similarly, when the children of the indifferent 'West End Jews' have passed the period when the example of parents is followed without question, when they begin to think for themselves, they realize that they have no religion. The majority accept, after a period of uncertainty, the conventional pretences of their parents, and adhere to them until they become inconvenient, when they cast them off altogether. Many of the young men and women have periods of intense craving for some definite faith, and would even return to the Ghetto-worship if their minds could admit its principles. Perhaps they have glimpses, which fill them with extreme joy and hope, of a revived and ennobling Judaism, which might become the guiding inspiration of their lives. A few retain these visions, and are continually cheered by them; a very few seek to realize them more closely; the many prefer to banish disquieting dreams; and in choosing for the hour peace of mind, cut off for ever real happiness – spiritual joy, the best of the gifts which God offers to his children.

In what way does the community attempt to meet the needs of its younger members, in whom the hope of Judaism in the future rests, and to stay the current of indifference which, both in the 'East End' and in the 'West End', is threatening its foundations? Among some of the better educated parents who are conscious of their responsibilities, there is noticeable an ominous bewilderment, when they consider what form of religious instruction they are to give to their children. If they send them to religious classes at the synagogues, or if they arrange for masters to give private instruction, the success of their efforts depends generally on the personal force and influence of the teachers. The children are further required to attend the synagogue services, but these have no hold over their growing life. As a rule, they are inattentive; and if they pray at all, it is that the prayers may speedily end. The occasional introduction of a children's sermon does not for them materially relieve the tedium of the service. A preacher who speaks to a mixed congregation of adults and children is generally self-conscious, and his words are often addressed to unresponsive minds. The children are humiliated by the seeming publicity of their faults, and irritated by the silent or whispered delight of their elders, when some pulpit rebuke is especially applicable to them.

Yet children are naturally religious.

On the other hand; the 'East End' parents are not satisfied that the instruction given by the Religious Education Board and the voluntary Sabbath-class teachers is adequate to satisfy the spiritual needs of their children, and at the educational conference the fact was generally deplored that these children were still further instructed out of school hours. It is still more deplorable that these very children, who have been subjected to this elaborate religious training, who have attended school and *cheder*, are found, when they have ceased to be students, and even during the period of their preparation, to be conscious of no anxiety to pray, of no sense that religion renders truthfulness and self-sacrifice obligatory. With some signal exceptions, the voluntary Sabbath-class teachers consider that they satisfy the claims of religion by insisting on extreme decorum in their class, and instructing it in the recital of prayers which are not felt or understood. The children are not awed by the grandeur of God, nor drawn to him by his love. They merely repeat a weekly lesson, which has become easy through iteration, and which can awaken no spiritual joy.

The members of the Religious Education Board are, doubtless, inspired by the highest motives. They would like to adopt the 'East End' religion, and to teach it in an intelligent and enlightened manner, showing that the greater part of the observances are estimable only as methods, never as objects of worship. But the members of the Board belong to the leisured classes, and seem unable to carry out their scheme by personal effort; their own religion is not the 'East End' religion, and they cannot impart a fervour for what they do not feel. They depute the work to others, who conscientiously teach religion as geography and history are taught. Consequently, although their pupils come to answer intelligently, the lessons they learn are not assimilated in a manner to influence their everyday life. Religion remains a subject to be noticed at certain specified times and seasons, but has no intimate connection with life's joys and cares.

The conditions of modern Judaism, then, from every point of view, present a grievous aspect to honest observers. In vain we seek to gloss over facts; in vain we point triumphantly to our charity-lists, to our learning, to our position in the front of every rank and profession. We yet have to confess ourselves unable to impart to our children a strengthening faith. Are we not also becoming every year more self-indulgent, more ostentatious, less reverent? Why is there a growing tendency among all classes of Jewish youth to forget the serious purposes of life, and to set the pleasures of gain, of dress, of food, of dancing, and of acting, above all else that is desirable on earth? Why do we gamble so much? Why do we grudge personal service in combating the moral evils of our day? Why is complete personal sacrifice to the needs of our poor so rare among us? Why do our philanthropists, even our ministers, forbear to introduce religion into their visiting work, unless to or about those who are about to leave this world? Why cannot we suppress the lying and deceit which flourish in our midst? Why do our friends and relatives marry out of the faith, passing among the Gentiles as freethinkers, upon whom religion has no claim? Why are the old laws, which kept the minds of our fathers in pious subservience, still preserved, seeing that here and there they require a sermon to justify their existence, and a sacrifice of truth to facilitate their observance?

The answer to these questions must be, that the highest Jewish influences are for the time being dormant, and have ceased to inspire our lives; that our belief in a supernatural law is only a verbal one, and that in spite of our professions we are stirred by no desire to prepare ourselves for a better spiritual state. Indeed, without some strong spiritual awakening, how can we hope to arrest our degenerate tendencies?

Yet, in spite of all these depressing facts, in spite of our present callousness and inertia, there is every reason for hope – for hope, glorious and infinite. If we examine our Judaism with a trusting spirit, we find that it still contains the germs of life; we find that its abiding essence is simplicity and truth. At present our thinkers are oppressed by the religious lethargy from which our age is just emerging. Only now and again a true believer appears in our midst, one who clings to his religion, and derives from it spiritual joy and a stimulus to moral progress; who sacrifices his own pleasure constantly in order to serve his fellows; who draws inspiration at all times from God and from his creations, because *his* Judaism impels it. The problem before us is how to restore confidence to our thinkers, and to encourage them to free our religion from the earth, which is clogging it, and to allow it to spread and to stimulate the lives of all generations. There is only one method by which we can hope to achieve these ends. *That method is association.*

When about the year 1840 the Italians became conscious of their state of subjection and determined to issue from it, Giuseppe Mazzini appealed to them to associate together in the service of God and of their country. He saw that only after self-regeneration could his countrymen hope to frustrate tyranny, and that only by association could they obtain the needful strength to execute the tasks before them. Whether it is left for generations yet unborn to inherit the glorious future which Mazzini predicted for his country, or whether the associated bands of young Italy are gone for ever and have left no trace, I still believe that the great Italian's teachings are fundamentally true. We Jews are suffering at home from the tyranny of spiritual sloth, and abroad from the tyranny of persecution. If we are to be free, Mazzini's powerful appeal for association should echo and re-echo in our midst. For his words may be applied to communities as well as to nations, to religious brotherhoods as well as to political states. He says, 'Association is a security for progress. The State represents a certain sum or mass of *principles* in which the universality of the citizens are agreed at the time of its foundation. Suppose that a new and true principle, a new and rational development of the truths that have given vitality to the State, should be discovered by a few among its citizens. How should they diffuse the knowledge of the principle except by association? Inertia and a disposition to rest satisfied with the order of things long existing, and sanctioned by the common consent, are habits too powerful over the minds of most men to allow a single individual to overcome them by his solitary word. The association of a daily increasing minority can do this. Association is the method of the future' (Mazzini, *Duties of Man*).

It is only by association that we can effectually enunciate the principle, that we are required to use in God's service all the gifts of mind and heart which he has granted to us, since it is a form of blasphemy to conceal or to pervert truth, in order to render our service of God acceptable to him. We, who are conscious of our great needs, must organize ourselves into an association to rediscover our Judaism, encouraging one another to reformulate our ideal. We shall be able to rally round us the discontented and weary, and together we may hope to lift Judaism from its desolate position and absorb it into our lives. Together we must sift with all reverence the pure from the impure in the laws which our ancestors formulated in order to satisfy the needs of their age, and refuse to resort to hairsplitting argument in order to reestablish a religion which was originally founded on a basis of truth, dignity and beauty. We must no longer grimly reiterate the fact that Judaism has ceased to appeal to us, and lack the energy to inquire into the cause of its degeneration. We must boldly follow Isaiah, Jeremiah and Ezekiel, and allow a place to progress in religious thought. Yet, at the outset of our search, we shall be persuaded that only the elect among us can worship at the 'Fount of Inspiration' without some assistance in the form of a ritualistic system, and that the perpetuation of Judaism therefore requires the maintenance of certain ceremonial observances. For the essence of a religion cannot be transmitted in all its simplicity to a child, whose mind cannot conceive an abstraction, and a certain discipline of observance is essential to character-training. We can only combat our tendency to self-indulgence and to spiritual sloth by having fasts and holydays reserved for communion with God. Inspired by a natural desire to examine with all tenderness the possessions, which our fathers preserved with so much courage and devotion, we shall probably find treasures of beauty and truth where we had expected deformity and deception. We shall then be able to assign to observances, which had been worshipped as the end, their proper place and function as means for the attainment of holiness.

Judaism once rediscovered, and our faith in its utility revived, we shall be able to undertake with better heart the instruction of our children. One of our first duties as an organized association must be to arrange children's services throughout the kingdom. We have to teach our children first to 'seek the Lord, while he may be found, to call upon him while he is near'; and, secondly, that our thoughts are not his thoughts, nor our ways his ways' (Isa. 45:6,8). We must make them realize that God is Love, and that human love which bridges life and death, is only a reflection of divine love, which reaches from heaven to earth. The lesson of God's omnipresence may be best enforced by a constant variety of service, and by the introduction of passing events and the incidents of daily life as themes for prayer. It might certainly be urged that a constantly varying service during childhood would render any fixed ritual irksome. But with the growth of judgment the necessity for some uniformity in worship will be felt. Our children have to learn that prayer involves *effort*. If they could see their leader moved by spiritual need, struggling to approach his God, they would unconsciously join in the search, and experience veneration in the presence of God. From the beginning, the value of prayer in combating vicious pleasures and the neglect of truth must be enforced. The children must learn that the active, conscious search after God cannot be confined to morning and evening prayer, nor begun and ended on Sabbaths and festivals. The believing Jew and Jewess must seek guidance from God in the morning, be conscious of his presence throughout the day, and pray for a renewed inspiration at night. Then Judaism will have gained through fervent prayer far more than it can have lost through less regard for form; and its professing followers will look to it once more to satisfy some definite need in their lives.

As an association, we must prove the utility of our religion by showing that it admits of endless development. We must prove that we are not a destructive body, and that we did not chafe because we required more ease; for while waging a crusade against deceit and impurity, we are only seeking to restore to Judaism its power over our lives. We must avoid all boasting and ostentation; even as our aim is high, so should our self-distrust be great. It is obvious how inadequate is our strength to achieve even a small part of the purpose we have in view, seeing that our generation, however united and zealous it may become, can only indicate the road which posterity may think it right to follow.

I have suggested the organization of an associated band of worshippers, bound together by the tenets of a living Judaism. It is possible to attempt a slight forecast of the lines on which such an association may work and its more immediate results. We may hope for the gradual abandonment of gambling and other vicious pleasures, the desire for a more simple life animated by love of truth and of piety, and an increase in the number and devotion of those who are ready to devote themselves to preventive rather than curative social work, and who would attempt relief by moral stimuli, as well as by material props. The present is the right hour, and England is the fit place for the initiation of this movement, which may restore to Judaism its glory.

In England Jews can freely develop all their powers, and follow, unquestioned, their ideals. If, then, the English Jews are better able than most of their continental brothers to recognize the potentiality of their spiritual inheritance, the obligation rests imperatively upon them to formulate its meaning and render it intelligible. By continuing to follow mechanically a religion which they have not the energy to revive, by maintaining tenets which jar on their sense of truth, they are neglecting their most urgent duties, and rendering themselves for ever unfit to serve their brothers. For we English Jews owe a duty to our less fortunate co-religionists, who are still suffering from the effects of persecution. In some countries we find Jews who have been denied the advantages of education, for whom persecution has tightened the spiritual bonds by causing them to build up a wall of observance effectually shutting out God's light. They are dimly conscious of a glorious inheritance transmitted to them by their fathers, and threatened by cruel and impious strangers. Too fearful to examine the nature of this inheritance, and to discover that its qualities defy the art of thieves, they fence it with rows of bulwarks constructed with pious ingenuity. Holy, is the aim of the persecuted; there is no schism or rebellion in their midst; they do not understand that their service has been gradually diverted from the Giver of all good to the ritual gods, who were originally raised on high for the purpose of his defence. But when persecution ceases, and men are freed from its effects, they will examine the nature of the ritual gods they have served so conscientiously. A revulsion of feeling, a horror at their long idolatry may follow; tradition may lose its purifying hold over their minds, and they may yield themselves up to licence, and call it intellectual emancipation. It is possible for us in England to avert this catastrophe. At the moment when our persecuted brethren are in their greatest need, when they realize the hollowness of their worship, they may be saved from spiritual anarchy if they see among us a religion comprising all that was valuable and lovely in the ancient faith, embodied in forms acceptable to emancipated minds.

In other countries we see Jews who, having once known intellectual freedom, are now denied the privilege of developing all their intellectual, social and material possessions, unless they submit to conditions which will rob them of their Judaism. For a long time they may refuse to accept these conditions, although, like their less enlightened brothers, they have probably not examined the purport of their religious inheritance. They are at present restrained from doing so by vanity rather than by piety, for they vaguely believe that their ancient faith, the source of so much of their fathers' glory, will not survive a severe scrutiny. Their attempts to suppress intelligence result in a lifeless form of worship, and, in all probability, the scruples which made the preservation of a religious system at all possible will gradually melt away before the claims of self-advancement. The religion which has long ceased to inspire love will be at last critically examined, and contempt for it will fill the minds of its former devotees; its merits over other religions will appear doubtful, and men will resolve no longer to cramp their own and their children's lives in its cause. Consideration for the children's happiness will probably be most potent in inducing the change to be made, and even if the state religion is not formally adopted, the old religion will no longer block the road to success.

These gloomy prophecies are warranted by many precedents in the history of continental Judaism; but I believe that, if in England we associate to maintain Jewish ideals, we shall be able to show by the gladness and the holiness of our lives that Judaism is worth *any* sacrifice. Then the persecuted will renew their courage, and be saved from deserting the religion whose value is proved before their eyes.

Surely we English Jews can have no excuse for continued indifference and waiting. To us the call is clear and unmistakable. For our own sakes we must revive Judaism, and having reconciled its dogma with our highest conception of truth and beauty, allow it again to bind us to the God who cares for us. In order to answer the challenge of the 'East End Jew', we must prove that our faith is no longer comatose, that we are truly striving after an ideal, and that we are ready to make any sacrifice that our religion may claim. For the sake of our foreign brothers, whose eyes are blinded by present misery from seeing the light which is within their reach, we English Jews must unite to strengthen our faith and proclaim the infinite hope contained within it.

There is everything to fear for the future of Judaism, until it can be accepted by the most enlightened among us. Better to have died in the Ghetto than to have outlived the possibilities of our religion. But surely there is no need for despair seeing that a broader and more beautiful worship, which will grow in intensity, as the needs of a more developed civilization become greater, can even now be dimly foreshadowed.

Some critics are fond of noticing the popularity of Ghetto, or hard-shelled, Jews among the Gentiles, and comparing it with the odium suffered by the unobservant Jews. We cannot hide from ourselves one reason at any rate for such a preference. The Ghetto Jews need not be feared as rivals, since their development is checked by laws of their own making, while the emancipated Jews are without binding laws, and therefore uncramped in their competition with their neighbours. The racial Jew, devoted to self-seeking and ostentation, and arrogant of his race, although destitute of spiritual faith, is indeed deserving of every scorn. His Judaism is not of his own seeking, and he consequently makes no sacrifice to follow it; he cherishes a materialistic ideal, which threatens the highest good of our age. It is the Jew who is a racial Jew only who must be helped to religious Judaism once more by being induced to join an association intent on proving the value of the religion for which his fathers lived and died. And if such a band, doing such glorious work, should reawaken intolerance among our neighbours, we are prepared to welcome martyrdom and to call it a joyous deliverance, seeing that it will have freed us from the lethargy which is at present oppressing our spirits. If, as is far more probable, we are able by a strongly organized religious movement to arrest our own spiritual degeneration and to revive our faith, that mission of the Lord's Servant unto the nations, which was the highest aspiration of the Second Isaiah, may even yet be turned from a vision into reality.

But before we Jews can claim to be a religious brotherhood, before we can pretend to possess a faith through which we can speak tidings of salvation and peace to all nations, we must be able to rest our title on our own efforts rather than on the accident of our birth. Whatever the creed of his father, whether Roman Catholic, Protestant or Jewish, a religious man must seek and discover God for himself. I believe that in Judaism will be found the methods by which God can be most surely approached, and that these methods are certain ultimately to prevail universally. But no fresh discovery can be made exactly on the lines of the past; the temperament of one generation differs from that of another, and life is only possible when it can adapt itself to environment. Let us dare to speak with courage to our brothers and sisters, and to our sons and daughters; let us bid them not hesitate in their search after the divine, because they use data and methods not already tried by their ancestors. Judaism is strong enough and wide enough to inspire them and their children for ever; let us ask them to make progressive demands upon it. Let us tell them indeed that they can *only* be Jews and Jewesses if they *do* live up to the ideals of truth and morality expounded by the best teachers of their age.[2]

NOTES

1. This article provided the cornerstone upon which the foundation of Liberal Judaism was based. More than any single piece of writing, 'The Spiritual Possibilities in Judaism Today' marked the beginning of a process that ultimately led to the establishment of Liberal Judaism in England. Lily Montagu's article, written and published at the behest of Claude Montefiore, needs to be read in its entirety, as it identifies the problems faced by Jews in England over one hundred years ago. Many of these problems exist today.
2. LM, *Jewish Quarterly Review* (1899), pp. 216–31.

Select Bibliography

WRITINGS BY ISRAEL ABRAHAMS

1895   *Aspects of Judaism* (with Claude Montefiore), London: Macmillan.
1896   *Jewish Life in the Middle Ages*, London: Macmillan.
1903   *Maimonides* (with David Yellin) London: Macmillan.
1906   *Festival Studies*, London: Macmillan.
1906   *A Short History of Jewish Literature*, London: T. Fisher & Unwin.
1907   *Judaism*, London: A. Constable & Co.
1912   *The Book of Delight*, Philadelphia: JPS.
        Annotated Edition of Authorised Daily Prayer Book, London: Eyre & Spottiswoode.
1917   *Studies in Pharisaism and the Gospels: First Series*, Cambridge: Cambridge University Press.
1920   *By-Paths in Hebraic Bookland*, Philadelphia: JPS.
1923   *Permanent Values in Judaism*, New York: Jewish Institute Press.
1924   *Studies in Pharisaism and the Gospels: Second Series*, Cambridge: Cambridge University Press.

WRITINGS ABOUT ISRAEL ABRAHAMS

Kohut, E. (ed.) (1927), *Jewish Studies in Memory of Israel Abrahams*, New York: Jewish Institute of Religion.
Levy, S. (1937), *Bibliography of 'IA': Dr Israel Abrahams 1858–1925*, London: Jewish Historical Society of England.
Hyamson, A. (1940), *Israel Abrahams: A Memoir*, London: JRU.
Loewe, H. (1944), *Israel Abrahams*, Cambridge: Arthur Davies Memorial Trust.

Horowitz, E. (1998), '*Jewish Life in the Middle Ages* and the Jewish life of Israel Abrahams', in D. Myers, and D. Ruderman (eds), *The Jewish Past Revisited: Reflections on Modern Jewish Historians* (New Haven, CT: Yale University Press), pp. 143–62.

WRITINGS BY CLAUDE MONTEFIORE

1892   *Hibbert Lectures on the Origin and Growth of Religion as Illustrated by the Ancient Hebrews*, London: Williams and Norgate.
1895   *Aspects of Judaism* (with Israel Abrahams), London: Macmillan.
1895   *The Bible for Home Reading*, London: Macmillan.
1903   *Liberal Judaism*, London: Macmillan.
1906   *Truth in Religion and Other Sermons*, London: Macmillan.
1910   *The Synoptic Gospels*, 2 vols, London: Macmillan.
1911   *Judaism and St Paul*, London: M. Goshen.
1912   *Outlines of Liberal Judaism*, London: Macmillan.
1918   *Liberal Judaism and Hellenism*, London: Macmillan.
1923   *The Old Testament and After*, London: Macmillan.
1930   *Rabbinic Literature and Gospel Teachings*, London: Macmillan.
1938   *A Rabbinic Anthology* (with Herbert Loewe), London: Macmillan.

WRITINGS ABOUT CLAUDE MONTEFIORE

Cohen, L. (1940), *Some Recollections of Claude Goldsmid Montefiore*, London: Faber and Faber.
Jacob, W. (1970), 'Claude Montefiore', *Judaism*, pp. 328–41.
Stein, J. (1988), *Liber Freund: The letters of Claude Goldsmid Montefiore to Solomon Schechter 1885–1902*, New York: University of America Press.
Kessler, E. (1989) (2nd edn 2002), *An English Jew: The life and writings of Claude Montefiore*, London: Vallentine Mitchell.
Langton, D. (2001), *The Life and Thought of Claude Montefiore*, London: Vallentine Mitchell.

WRITINGS BY LILY MONTAGU

1899   'The Spiritual Possibilities of Judaism Today', *JQR* 11, pp. 216–31.
1901   *Naomi's Exodus: A tale*, London: T. Fisher & Unwin.
1902   *Broken Stalks*, London: R. Brimley Johnson.
1904   *Thoughts on Judaism*, London: R. Brimley Johnson.
1904   'The Girl in the Background' in E. J. Urwick, *Studies of Boy Life in Our Cities*, London: J. M. Dent, pp. 233–54.
1926   *What Can A Mother Do?* London: Routledge & Sons.
1941   *My Club and I: The Story of The West Central Jewish Club*, London: Herbert Joseph.
1943   *The Faith of a Jewish Woman*, London: G. Allen & Unwin.
1944   *Suggestions for Sabbath Eve Celebrations* (2nd edn) London: Wightman & Co.
1946   *A Little Book of Comfort for Jewish People in Times of Sorrow* (with R. Brasch), London: Wightman & Co.

WRITINGS ABOUT LILY MONTAGU

Conrad, E. (1953), *Lily H. Montagu: Prophet of a Living Judaism*, New York: National Federation of Temple Sisterhoods.

(1963), *Liberal Jewish Monthly, Memorial*, March 1963, London.

— (ed.) (1967), *In Memory of Lily H. Montagu: Some Extracts From Her Letters and Addresses*, Amsterdam: Polak and Van Gennep.

Levy, N. G. (1968), *The West Central Story and its Founders: The Hon. Lily H. Montagu CBE, JP, DD and the Hon. Marian Montagu, 1893–1968*, London.

Umansky, E. (1983), *Lily Montagu and the Advancement of Liberal Judaism* (Studies in Women and Religion, Vol. 13), New York: Edwin Mellen.

— (1985), *Lily Montagu: Sermons, Addresses and Prayers* (Studies in Women and Religion, Vol. 15), New York: Edwin Mellen.

WRITINGS BY ISRAEL MATTUCK

1918   *Services and Prayers for Jewish Homes*, London: JRU.
1923–26 *Liberal Jewish Prayer Book* (3 vols), London: JRU.
1937   *Faith and the Modern World*, London: JRU.

1939   *What are the Jews?*, London: Hodder & Stoughton.
1947   *The Essentials of Liberal Judaism*, London: Routledge & Sons.
1953   *Jewish Ethics*, London: Hutchinson.
1953   *The Thoughts of the Prophets*, London:
1954   *Aspects of Progressive Judaism*, London: Gollancz.

WRITINGS ABOUT ISRAEL MATTUCK

Liberal Jewish Monthly (memorial number, June 1954).
Jewish Chronicle (9 April 1954).
Rayner, J. D. R. (1993), 'Rabbi Israel Mattuck: a man of the past – and the future?', *Manna*.